The Big Book of Crochet Sweaters

Bobbie Matela, Managing Editor

Carol Wilson Mansfield, Art Director

Mary Ann Frits, Editorial Director

Kathy Wesley, Pattern Editor

Stephanie Hill, Kelly Robinson and Sandy Scoville, Editorial Staff

Kathryn Smith, Assistant Editor

Graphic Solutions inc-chgo, Book Design

*For a full-color catalog including books
of knit and crochet designs, write to:*

American School of Needlework®
Consumer Division
1455 Linda Vista Drive
San Marcos, CA 92069

We wish to thank the following for providing yarn for our sweaters: Coats and Clark; Lion Brand® Yarns; Patons; Elmore-Pisgah, Inc.; and Spinrite®, Inc.

Patterns tested and models made by Marianne Forrestal, Mary Ann Frits, Viola Oldland, Carly Poggemeyer, Kelly Robinson, and Pat Yankee.

We have made every effort to ensure the accuracy and completeness of these instructions. We cannot, however, be responsible for human error, typographical mistakes, or variations in individual work.

Introduction

When it comes to sweaters, the more the better! We love sweaters for all seasons and reasons, in a variety of colors, textures, shapes, and sizes.

If you share our affection for sweaters, you'll adore this diverse batch of fashionable crocheted sweaters. Tunics, cardigans, and pullovers, both long- and short-sleeved, are among the ten designer sweaters presented in this book of smart styles and step-by-step patterns.

Distinctive stitches, like shells, scallops, and popcorns, add texture and flair to these lovely tops crocheted in popular cotton, wool, and chenille yarns.

Contents

Abbreviations and Symbols

Crochet Abbreviations

beg	begin(ning)
BL(s)	back loop(s)
BPdc	back post double crochet(s)
ch(s)	chain(s)
CL(s)	cluster(s)
dc	double crochet(s)
dec	decrease(-ing)
FL(s)	front loop(s)
FPdc	front post double crochet(s)
hdc	half double crochet(s)
inc	increase(-ing)
lp(s)	loop(s)
patt	pattern
PC(s)	popcorn(s)
prev	previous
rem	remain(ing)
rep	repeat(ing)
rnd(s)	round(s)
sc	single crochet(s)
sk	skip
sl	slip
sl st(s)	slip stitch(es)
sp(s)	space(s)
st(s)	stitch(es)
tog	together
trc	triple crochet(s)
YO	yarn over

* An asterisk is used to mark the beginning of a portion of instructions to be worked more than once; thus, "rep from ***** twice more" means after working the instructions once, repeat the instructions following the asterisk twice more (3 times in all).

† The dagger identifies a portion of instructions that will be repeated again later in the same row.

—The number after a long dash at the end of a row indicates the number of stitches you should have when the row has been completed.

() Parentheses are used to enclose instructions which should be worked the exact number of times specified immediately following the parentheses, such as "(2 sc in next dc, sc in next dc) twice." They are also used to set off and clarify a group of stitches that are to be worked all into the same space or stitch, such as "(2 dc, ch 1, 2 dc) in corner sp."

[ ] Brackets and **()** parentheses are also used to provide additional information to clarify instructions.

Join - join with a sl st unless otherwise specified.

Terms

Right or Wrong?

We use these words in several different ways.

Right Side of the garment means the side that will be seen when it is worn.

Wrong Side of the garment means the side that will be inside when it is worn.

Right Front means the part of the garment that will be worn on the right front.

Left Front means the part of the garment that will be worn on the left front.

Continue in Pattern as Established is usually used in a pattern stitch, and this means to continue following the pattern stitch as it is already set up (established), working any subsequent increases or decreases (usually, worked at the beginning or end of a row) in such a way that the established pattern remains the same.

Work Even means to continue to work in the pattern as established, without working any increases or decreases.

The patterns in this book are written using United States terminology. Terms which have different English equivalents are noted below.

United States	English
single crochet (sc)	double crochet (dc)
half double crochet (hdc)	half treble (htr)
double crochet (dc)	treble (tr)
triple crochet (trc)	double treble (dtr)
skip (sk)	miss
slip stitch (sl st)	slip stitch (ss) or "single crochet"
gauge	tension
yarn over (YO)	yarn over hook (YOH)

Stitch Guide

Chain - ch:
YO, draw through lp on hook.

Single Crochet - sc:
Insert hook in st, YO and draw through, YO and draw through both lps on hook.

Reverse Single Crochet -
Reverse sc:
Work from left to right, insert hook in sp or st indicated (**a**), draw lp through sp or st - 2 lps on hook (**b**); YO and draw through lps on hook.

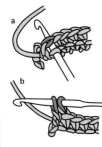

Half Double Crochet - hdc:
YO, insert hook in st, YO, draw through, YO and draw through all 3 lps on hook.

Double Crochet - dc:
YO, insert hook in st, YO, draw through, (YO and draw through 2 lps on hook) twice.

Triple Crochet - trc:
YO twice, insert hook in st, YO, draw through, (YO and draw through 2 lps on hook) 3 times.

Slip Stitch - sl st:
(a) **Used for Joinings**
Insert hook in indicated st, YO and draw through st and lp on hook.

(b) **Used for Moving Yarn Over**
Insert hook in st, YO draw through st and lp on hook.

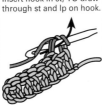

Front Loop - FL:
The front loop is the loop toward you at the top of the stitch.

Back Loop - BL:
The back loop is the loop away from you at the top of the stitch.

Post:
The post is the vertical part of the stitch.

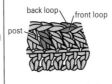

back loop

front loop

post

Overcast Stitch is worked loosely to join crochet pieces.

Following Size in Patterns

The patterns include sizes from small to large. Each pattern is written for the smallest size with changes in number of stitches (or inches) for other sizes in parentheses. For example, the pattern will tell you how many chains you need to start as follows:

Ch 20 **(23, 24)**.

You would chain 20 for the small size, 23 for medium, or 24 for large. We suggest that before you begin crocheting, you highlight or circle all the numbers throughout the pattern for the size you are making.

A Word about the Yarns

These beautiful sweaters have been created using the following yarns: Lion Brand® Micro Spun and Wool Ease®; Coats and Clark Southmaid Cotton 8; Honeysuckle Yarns Rayon Chenille; Sprinrite® Lily® Sugar 'n Cream Sport; Patons Cotton d.k.; and Tahki Imports' Cotton Classic. Each of our pattterns specifies the yarn we used for our photographed sweaters, but you may choose to substitute yarn of the same weight that will work to the same gauge.

A Word about Gauge

A correct stitch gauge is very important. Please take the time to work a stitch gauge swatch about 4" x 4". Measure the swatch. If the number of stitches and rows are fewer than indicated under "Gauge" in the pattern, your hook is too large. Try another swatch with a smaller size hook. If the number of stitches and rows are more than indicated under "Gauge" in the pattern, your hook is too small. Try another swatch with a larger size hook.

Metric Charts

INCHES INTO MILLIMETERS & CENTIMETERS (Rounded off slightly)

inches	mm	cm	inches	cm	inches	cm	inches	cm
1/8	3		5	12.5	21	53.5	38	96.5
1/4	6		5 1/2	14	22	56	39	99
3/8	10	1	6	15	23	58.5	40	101.5
1/2	13	1.3	7	18	24	61	41	104
5/8	15	1.5	8	20.5	25	63.5	42	106.5
3/4	20	2	9	23	26	66	43	109
7/8	22	2.2	10	25.5	27	68.5	44	112
1	25	2.5	11	28	28	71	45	114.5
1 1/4	32	3.2	12	30.5	29	73.5	46	117
1 1/2	38	3.8	13	33	30	76	47	119.5
1 3/4	45	4.5	14	35.5	31	79	48	122
2	50	5	15	38	32	81.5	49	124.5
2 1/2	65	6.5	16	40.5	33	84	50	127
3	75	7.5	17	43	34	86.5		
3 1/2	90	9	18	46	35	89		
4	100	10	19	48.5	36	91.5		
4 1/2	115	11.5	20	51	37	94		

mm - millimeter   cm - centimeter

CROCHET HOOKS CONVERSION CHART

U.S.	1/B	2/C	3/D	4/E	5/F	6/G	8/H	9/I	10/J	10 1/2/K	N
Continental-mm	2.25	2.75	3.25	3.5	3.75	4.25	5	5.5	6	6.5	9.0

Career Cardigan

designed by Hélène Rush

Sizes:

	Small	Medium	Large
Chest Measurement:	30"-32"	34"-36"	38"-40"
Finished Chest Measurement:	38"	40"	42"

Note: Instructions are written for size small; changes for larger sizes are in parentheses.

Materials:

Lion Brand Micro Spun (2.5 oz skein), 3 (4, 4) skeins Ebony #153; 3 (3, 4) skeins Cherry Red #113; 3 (3, 4) skeins Lily White #100—or other sport weight yarn worked to gauge
Size H (5mm) crochet hook or size required for gauge
Seven ⅝" diameter black buttons
Sewing needle and matching thread
Size 16 tapestry needle

Gauge:

Note: See "A Word about Gauge" on page 5.
4 dc = 1"
2 dc rows = 1"
In pattern:
16 sts = 4"
14 rows = 4"

All measurements are approximate.

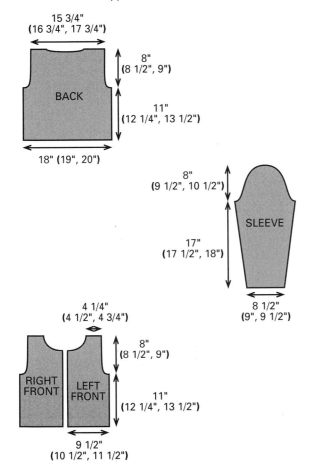

Instructions

Note: When changing color at end of row, work until 2 lps of last st rem on hook; with new color, YO and draw through 2 lps on hook. Cut old color.

Back

With black, ch 74 (78, 82).

Row 1 (right side):
Sc in 2nd ch from hook and in each rem ch—73 (77, 81) sc. Ch 3 (counts as first dc on following rows), turn.

Row 2:
Sk first sc, dc in next 3 sc; * ch 1, sk next sc, dc in next 3 sc; rep from * 16 (17, 18) times more; dc in next sc, changing to red. Ch 1, turn.

Row 3:
Sc in first 4 dc; * working over next ch-1 sp, sc in next skipped sc on 2nd row below, sc in next 3 sc; rep from * 16 (17, 18) times more; sc in 3rd ch of turning ch-3. Ch 3, turn.

Row 4:
Sk first sc, dc in next sc; * ch 1, sk next sc, dc in next 3 sc; rep from * 16 (17, 18) times more; ch 1, sk next sc, dc in next 2 sc, changing to white in last dc. Ch 1, turn.

continued

Color photograph, page 34

Row 5:
Sc in first 2 dc; * † working over next ch-1 sp, sc in next skipped sc on 2nd row below †; sc in next 3 dc; rep from * 16 (17, 18) times more, then rep from † to † once; sc in next dc and in 3rd ch of turning ch-3. Ch 3, turn.

Row 6:
Rep Row 2, changing to black in last dc. Ch 1, turn.

Rows 7 and 8:
Rep Rows 3 and 4, changing to red in last dc of Row 8. Ch 1, turn.

Row 9:
Rep Row 5.

Row 10:
Rep Row 2, changing to white in last dc. Ch 1, turn.

Rows 11 and 12:
Rep Rows 3 and 4, changing to black in last dc of Row 12. Ch 1, turn.

Row 13:
Rep Row 5.

Rows 14 through 37:
Rep Rows 2 through 13 twice more.

Rows 38 through 39 (43, 47):
Rep Rows 2 through 3 (7, 11). At end of Row 39 (43, 47), do not ch 3. Turn.

Armhole Shaping:
Note: Continue in color sequence as established.

Row 1 (wrong side):
Sl st in first 5 sts, ch 3 (counts as a dc), work in pattern as established to last 4 sts. Ch 1, turn, leaving rem sts unworked—65 (69, 73) dc.

Row 2 (right side):
Sc in first dc, dec over next 2 sts (to work dec: draw up lp in each of next 2 sts, YO, draw through all 3 lps on hook—dec made); work in patt to last 3 sts; dec; sc in 3rd ch of beg ch-3—63 (67, 71) sc. Ch 3, turn.

Row 3:
Sk first sc, dc dec over next 2 sc [to work dc dec: (YO, draw up lp in next st, YO, draw through 2 lps on hook) twice; YO and draw through all 3 lps on hook—dc dec made]; work in patt to last 3 sc; dc dec over next 2 sc; dc in last sc—61 (65, 69) dc. Ch 1, turn.

Row 4:
Sc in first dc, dec; work in patt to last 3 sts; dec; sc in 3rd ch of turning ch-3—59 (63, 67) sc. Ch 3, turn.

Row 5:
Sk first dc, dc dec; work in patt to last 3 sc; dc dec; dc in last sc—57 (61, 65) dc. Ch 1, turn.

Rows 6 through 28 (30, 32):
Work even in pattern and color sequence as established. At end of Row 28 (30, 32), finish off.

Left Front
With black, ch 38 (42, 46).

Row 1 (right side):
Sc in 2nd ch from hook and in each rem ch—37 (41, 45) sc. Ch 3 (counts as first dc on following rows), turn.

Row 2:
Sk first sc, dc in next sc; * ch 1, sk next sc, dc in next 3 sc; rep from * 7 (8, 9) times more; ch 1, sk next sc, dc in next 2 sc, changing to red in last dc. Ch 1, turn.

Row 3:
Sc in first 2 dc; * † working over next ch-1 sp, sc in next skipped sc on 2nd row below †; sc in next 3 dc; rep from * 7 (8, 9) times more, then rep from † to † once; sc in next dc and in 3rd ch of turning ch-3. Ch 3, turn.

Row 4:
Sk first sc, dc in next 3 sc; * ch 1, sk next sc, dc in next 3 sc; rep from * 7 (8, 9) times more; dc in next sc, changing to white. Ch 1, turn.

Row 5:
Sc in first 4 dc; * working over next ch-1 sp, sc in next skipped sc on 2nd row below, sc in next 3 dc; rep from * 7 (8, 9) times more; sc in 3rd ch of turning ch-3. Ch 3, turn.

Row 6:
Rep Row 2, changing to black in last dc. Ch 1, turn.

Rows 7 and 8:
Rep Rows 3 and 4, changing to red in last dc of Row 8. Ch 1, turn.

Row 9:
Rep Row 5.

Row 10:
Rep Row 2, changing to white in last dc. Ch 1, turn.

Rows 11 and 12:
Rep Rows 3 and 4, changing to black in last dc of Row 12. Ch 1, turn.

Row 13:
Rep Row 5.

Rows 14 through 37:
Rep Rows 2 through 13 twice more.

Rows 38 through 39 (43, 47):
Rep Rows 2 through 3 (7, 11).

Armhole Shaping:
Note: Continue in color sequence as established.

Row 1 (wrong side):
Work in patt as established to last 4 sts. Ch 1, turn, leaving rem sts unworked.

Row 2 (right side):
Sc in first dc, dec; work in patt across—32 (36, 40) sc. Ch 3, turn.

Row 3:
Work in patt to last 3 sts; dc dec; dc in last sc. Ch 1, turn.

Row 4:
Sc in first dc, dec; work in patt across—30 (34, 38) sc. Ch 3, turn.

Row 5:
Work in patt to last 3 sts; dc dec; dc in last sc. Ch 1, turn.

Rows 6 through 18 (20, 22):
Work even in pattern and color sequence as established.

Neck Shaping:
FOR SIZE SMALL ONLY:
Row 19 (wrong side**):**
SI st in first 8 sts, ch 3 (counts as a dc), work in patt across—22 sts. Ch 1, turn.

Row 20 (right side**):**
Work in patt to last 3 sts; dec; sc in 3rd ch of beg ch-3—21 sc. Ch 3, turn.

Row 21:
Dc dec; work in patt across. Ch 1, turn.

Row 22:
Work in patt to last 3 sts; dec; sc in 3rd ch of turning ch-3—19 sc. Ch 3, turn.

Row 23:
Rep Row 21.

Row 24:
Rep Row 20—17 sc.

Rows 25 through 28:
Work even in pattern and color sequence as established. At end of Row 28, finish off.

FOR SIZE MEDIUM ONLY:
Row 21 (wrong side**):**
SI st first 10 sts, ch 3 (counts as a dc), work in patt across—24 sts. Ch 1, turn.

Row 22 (right side**):**
Work in patt to last 3 sts; dec; sc in 3rd ch of beg ch-3—23 sc. Ch 3, turn.

Row 23:
Dc dec; work in patt across. Ch 1, turn.

Row 24:
Work in patt to last 3 sts; dec; sc in 3rd ch of turning ch-3—21 sc.

Row 25:
Dc dec; work in patt across. Ch 1, turn.

Rows 26 and 27:
Rep Rows 24 and 25.

Rows 28 through 30:
Work even in pattern and color sequence as established. At end of Row 30, finish off.

FOR SIZE LARGE ONLY:
Row 23 (wrong side**):**
SI st in first 12 sts, ch 3 (counts as a dc), work in patt across. Ch 1, turn.

Row 24 (right side**):**
Work in patt to last 3 sts; dec; sc in 3rd ch of beg ch-3—25 sc. Ch 3, turn.

Row 25:
Dc dec; work in patt across. Ch 1, turn.

Row 26:
Work in patt to last 3 sts; dec; sc in 3rd ch of turning ch-3—23 sc. Ch 3, turn.

Row 27:
Dc dec; work in patt across. Ch 1, turn.

Rows 28 and 29:
Rep Rows 26 and 27. At end of Row 29—20 sts.

Row 30:
Rep Row 26—19 sc.

Rows 31 and 32:
Work even in pattern and color sequence as established. At end of Row 32, finish off.

Right Front
Work as for Left Front to Armhole Shaping.

Armhole Shaping:
Note: Continue in color sequence as established.

Row 1 (wrong side**):**
SI st in first 5 sts, ch 3 (counts as a dc), work in patt across—33 (37, 41) sts. Ch 1, turn.

Row 2 (right side**):**
Work in patt to last 3 sts; dec; sc in 3rd ch of beg ch-3—32, (36, 40) sc. Ch 3, turn.

Row 3:
Dc dec; work in patt across. Ch 1, turn.

Row 4:
Work in patt to last 3 sts; dec; sc in 3rd ch of turning ch-3—30 (34, 38) sc. Ch 3, turn.

Row 5:
Dc dec; work in patt across. Ch 1, turn.

Rows 6 through 18 (20, 22):
Work even in pattern and color sequence as established.

Neck Shaping:
FOR SIZE SMALL ONLY:
Row 19 (wrong side**):**
Work in patt to last 7 sts. Ch 1, turn, leaving rem sts unworked.

continued

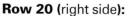

Row 20 (right side):
Sc in first sc, dec; work in patt across—21 sc. Ch 3, turn.

Row 21:
Work in patt to last 3 sc; dc dec; dc in last sc. Ch 1, turn.

Rows 22 and 23:
Rep Rows 20 and 21. At end of Row 23—18 sts.

Row 24:
Rep Row 20—17 sc.

Rows 25 through 28:
Work even in pattern and color sequence as established. At end of Row 28, finish off.

FOR SIZE MEDIUM ONLY:
Row 21 (wrong side):
Work in patt to last 9 sts. Ch 1, turn, leaving rem sts unworked.

Row 22 (right side):
Sc in first dc, dec; work in patt across—23 sc. Ch 3, turn.

Row 23:
Work in patt to last 3 sts; dc dec; dc in last st. Ch 1, turn.

Rows 24 through 27:
Rep Rows 22 and 23 twice more. At end of Row 27—18 sts.

Rows 28 through 30:
Work even in pattern and color sequence as established. At end of Row 30, finish off.

FOR SIZE LARGE ONLY:
Row 23 (wrong side):
Work in patt to last 11 sts. Ch 1, turn, leaving rem sts unworked.

Row 24 (right side):
Sc in first dc, dec; work in patt across—25 sc. Ch 3, turn.

Row 25:
Work in patt to last 3 sts; dc dec; dc in last sc. Ch 1, turn.

Rows 26 through 29:
Rep Rows 24 and 25 twice more. At end of Row 29—20 sts.

Row 30:
Rep Row 24—19 sc.

Rows 31 and 32:
Work even in pattern and color sequence as established. At end of Row 32, finish off.

Sleeve (make 2)

For Sizes Small and Medium Only:
With black, ch 34 (38).

Row 1 (right side):
Sc in 2nd ch from hook and in each rem ch—33 (37) sc. Ch 3 (counts as first dc on following rows), turn.

Row 2:
Sk first sc, dc in next 3 sc; * ch 1, sk next sc, dc in next 3 sc; rep from * 6 (7) times more; dc in next sc, changing to red. Ch 1, turn.

Row 3:
Sc in first 4 dc; * working over next ch-1 sp, sc in next skipped sc on 2nd row below, sc in next 3 dc; rep from * 6 (7) times more; sc in 3rd ch of turning ch-3. Ch 3, turn.

Row 4:
Sk first sc, dc in next sc; * ch 1, sk next sc, dc in next 3 sc; rep from * 6 (7) times more; ch 1, sk next sc, dc in next 2 sc, changing to white in last dc. Ch 1, turn.

Row 5:
2 sc in first dc; sc in next dc; * † working over next ch-1 sp, sc in next skipped sc on 2nd row below †; sc in next 3 dc; rep from * 6 (7) times more, then rep from † to † once; sc in next dc, 2 sc in 3rd ch of turning ch-3—35 (39) sc. Ch 4 (counts as first dc and ch-1 sp on following rows), turn.

Row 6:
Sk first 2 sc, dc in next 3 sc; * ch 1, sk next sc, dc in next 3 sc; rep from * 6 (7) times more; ch 1, sk next sc, dc in next sc, changing to black. Ch 1, turn.

Row 7:
Sc in first dc; * working over next ch-1 sp, sc in next skipped sc on 2nd row below, sc in next 3 dc; rep from * 7 (8) times more; working over next ch of turning ch-4, sc in next skipped sc on 2nd row below, sc in next ch of turning ch. Ch 3, turn.

Row 8:
Sk first sc, dc in next 2 sc; * ch 1, sk next sc, dc in next 3 sc; rep from * 7 (8) times more, changing to red in last dc. Ch 1, turn.

Row 9:
2 sc in first dc; sc in next 2 dc; * † working over next ch-1 sp, sc in next skipped sc on 2nd row below †; sc in next 3 dc; rep from * 6 (7) times more, then rep from † to † once; sc in next 2 dc, 2 sc in 3rd ch of turning ch-3—37 (41) sc. Ch 3, turn.

Row 10:
Sk first sc, dc in next sc; * ch 1, sk next sc, dc in next 3 sc; rep from * 7 (8) times more; ch 1, sk next sc, dc in next 2 sc, changing to white in last dc. Ch 1, turn.

Row 11:
Sc in first 2 dc; * † working over next ch-1 sp, sc in next skipped sc on 2nd row below †; sc in next 3 dc; rep from * 7 (8) times more, then rep from † to † once; sc in next dc and in 3rd ch of turning ch-3. Ch 3, turn.

Row 12:
Sk first sc, dc in next 3 sc; * ch 1, sk next sc, dc in next 3 sc; rep from * 7 (8) times more; dc in next sc, changing to black. Ch 1, turn.

Row 13:
Sc in first 4 dc; * working over next ch-1 sp, sc in next skipped sc on 2nd row below, sc in next 3 dc; rep from * 7 (8) times more; sc in 3rd ch of turning ch-3. Ch 3, turn.

Row 14:
Sk first sc, dc in next sc; * ch 1, sk next sc, dc in next 3 sc; rep from * 7 (8) times more; ch 1, sk next sc, dc in next 2 sc, changing to red in last dc. Ch 1, turn.

Row 15:
2 sc in first dc; sc in next dc; * † working over next ch-1 sp, sc in next skipped sc on 2nd row below †; sc in next 3 dc; rep from * 7 (8) times more, then rep from † to † once; sc in next dc, 2 sc in 3rd ch of turning ch-3— 39 (43) sc. Ch 4, turn.

Row 16:
Sk first 2 sc, dc in next 3 sc; * ch 1, sk next sc, dc in next 3 sc; rep from * 7 (8) times more; ch 1, sk next sc, dc in next sc, changing to white. Ch 1, turn.

Row 17:
Sc in first dc; * working over next ch-1 sp, sc in next skipped sc on 2nd row below, sc in next 3 dc; rep from * 8 (9) times more; working over next ch of turning ch-4, sc in next skipped sc on 2nd row below, sc in next ch of turning ch. Ch 3, turn.

Row 18:
Sk first sc, dc in next 2 sc; * ch 1, sk next sc, dc in next 3 sc; rep from * 8 (9) times more, changing to black in last dc. Ch 1, turn.

Row 19:
Sc in first 3 dc; * † working over next ch-1 sp, sc in next skipped sc on 2nd row below †; sc in next 3 dc; rep from * 7 (8) times more, then rep from † to † once; sc in next 2 dc and in 3rd ch of turning ch-3. Ch 4, turn.

Row 20:
Sk first 2 sc, dc in next 3 sc; * ch 1, sk next sc, dc in next 3 sc; rep from * 7 (8) times more; ch 1, sk next sc, dc in next sc, changing to red in last dc. Ch 1, turn.

Row 21:
2 sc in first dc; * working over next ch-1 sp, sc in next skipped sc on 2nd row below, sc in next 3 dc; rep from * 8 (9) times more; working over next ch of turning ch-4, sc in next skipped sc on 2nd row below, 2 sc in next ch of turning ch—41 (45) sc. Ch 3, turn.

Note: On following rows, work added sts as sc on right side rows and dc on wrong side rows until they can be incorporated into pattern.

Rows 22 through 57:
Continue in pattern and color sequence as established, inc one st at each end of every 6th row 6 times more. At end of Row 57—53 (57) sts.

Rows 58 through 59 (61):
Work even in pattern and color sequence as established. At end of Row 59 (61), do not ch 3. Turn.

Continue with Sleeve Cap Shaping on page 12.

For Size Large Only:
With black, ch 42.

Row 1 (right side):
Sc in 2nd ch from hook and in each rem ch—41 sc. Ch 3 (counts as first dc on following rows), turn.

Row 2:
Sk first sc, dc in next 3 sc; * ch 1, sk next sc, dc in next 3 sc; rep from * 8 times more; dc in next sc, changing to red. Ch 1, turn.

Row 3:
Sc in first 4 dc; * working over next ch-1 sp, sc in next skipped sc on 2nd row below, sc in next 3 dc; rep from * 8 times more; sc in 3rd ch of turning ch-3. Ch 3, turn.

Row 4:
Sk first sc, dc in next sc; * ch 1, sk next sc, dc in next 3 sc; rep from * 8 times more; ch 1, sk next sc, dc in next 2 sc, changing to white in last dc. Ch 1, turn.

Row 5:
Sc in first 2 dc; * † working over next ch-1 sp, sc in next skipped sc on 2nd row below †; sc in next 3 dc; rep from * 8 times more, then rep from † to † once; sc in next dc and in 3rd ch of turning ch-3. Ch 3, turn.

Row 6:
Rep Row 2, changing to black in last dc. Ch 1, turn.

Row 7:
2 sc in first dc; sc in next 3 dc; * working over next ch-1 sp, sc in next skipped sc on 2nd row below, sc in next 3 dc; rep from * 8 times more; 2 sc in 3rd ch of turning ch-3—43 sc. Ch 3, turn.

Row 8:
Sk first sc, dc in next 2 sc; * ch 1, sk next sc, dc in next 3 sc; rep from * 9 times more, changing to red in last dc. Ch 1, turn.

Row 9:
Sc in first 3 dc; * † working over next ch-1 sp, sc in next skipped sc on 2nd row below †; sc in next 3 dc; rep from * 8 times more, then rep from † to † once; sc in next 2 dc and in 3rd ch of turning ch-3. Ch 4 (counts as first dc and ch-1 sp on following rows), turn.

Row 10:
Sk first 2 sc, dc in next 3 sc; * ch 1, sk next sc, dc in next 3 sc; rep from * 8 times more; ch 1, sk next sc, dc in next sc, changing to white. Ch 1, turn.

Row 11:
Sc in first dc; * working over next ch-1 sp, sc in next skipped sc on 2nd row below, sc in next 3 dc; rep from * 9 times more; working over next ch of turning ch-4, sc in next skipped sc of 2nd row below, sc in next ch of turning ch. Ch 3, turn.

continued

11

Row 12:
Rep Row 8, changing to black in last dc. Ch 1, turn.

Row 13:
2 sc in first dc; sc in next 2 dc; * † working over next ch-1 sp, sc in next skipped sc on 2nd row below †; sc in next 3 dc; rep from * 8 times more, then rep from † to † once; sc in next 2 dc, 2 sc in 3rd ch of turning ch-3—45 sc. Ch 3, turn.

Note: On following rows, work added sts as sc on right side rows and dc on wrong side rows until they can be incorporated into pattern.

Rows 14 through 55:
Continue in pattern and color sequence as established, inc one st at each end of every 6th row 7 times more. At end of Row 55—59 sts.

Rows 56 through 63:
Work even in pattern and color sequence as established. At end of Row 63, do not ch 3. Turn.

Continue with Sleeve Cap Shaping.

Sleeve Cap Shaping:
Note: Continue in color sequence as established.

Row 1 (wrong side):
Sl st in first 5 sts, ch 3 (counts as a dc), work in patt to last 4 sts—45 (49, 51) sts. Turn, leaving rem sts unworked.

Row 2 (right side):
Sc in first dc, dec; work in patt to last 3 sts; dec; sc in 3rd ch of beg ch-3. Ch 3, turn.

Row 3:
Work in patt across. Ch 1, turn.

Row 4:
Sc in first dc, dec; work in patt to last 3 sts; dec; sc in 3rd ch of turning ch-3. Ch 3, turn.

Row 5:
Work in patt across. Ch 1, turn.

Rows 6 through 11 (17, 21):
Rep Rows 4 and 5, 3 (6, 8) times more.

Next Row:
Sc in first dc, dec; work in patt to last 3 sts; dec; sc in 3rd ch of turning ch-3. Ch 3, turn.

Next Row:
Sk first sc, dc dec; work in patt to last 3 sts; dc dec; dc in last sc. Ch 1, turn.

Rep last 2 rows until 7 sts rem. At end of last row, do not ch 1. Finish off.

Sew shoulder seams, beginning at armhole edge, matching corresponding stitches and leaving center 23 (25, 27) sts unworked for neck opening. Weave in all ends.

Front and Neck Band
With right side of Right Front facing you and with black, make lp on hook and join with an sc in edge st of Row 1 at lower edge of Right Front.

Row 1 (right side):
Sc in same sp as joining; working along right front edge in sps formed by edge sts and turning chs, sc in edge of each of next 56 (62, 68) rows; working along neck edge, 3 sc in first st (mark 2nd sc for corner), sc in next 7 (9, 11) sts; working along right neck edge in sps formed by edge sts and turning chs, sc in next 10 (10, 10) rows; working across back neck edge, sc in next 23 (25, 27) unworked sts; working along left neck edge in sps formed by edge sts and turning chs, sc in next 10 (10, 10) rows; working across front neck edge, sc in next 7 (9, 11) sts, 3 sc in next st (mark 2nd sc for corner); working along left front edge in sps formed by edge sts and turning chs, sc in each of next 57 (63, 69) rows—177 (195, 213) sc. Ch 1, turn.

Row 2:
Sc in each sc. Ch 1, turn.

Mark placement of 7 buttonholes evenly spaced on right front edge, placing first buttonhole 1½" from lower edge and seventh buttonhole at neck edge.

Row 3:
Sc in first sc; * sc in each sc to next marker; ch 2—buttonhole made; sk next 2 sc; rep from * 6 times more; sc in each sc to next marked sc; 3 sc in marked st (remark 2nd st for corner); sc in each sc to next marker; 3 sc in marked st (remark 2nd st for corner); sc in each rem sc. Ch 1, turn.

Row 4:
Sc in each sc to marked sc; 3 sc in marked sc; sc in each sc to next marked sc; 3 sc in marked sc; * sc in each sc to next ch-2 sp; 2 sc in ch-2 sp; rep from * 6 times more; sc in each rem sc. Ch 1, turn.

Row 5:
Sc in each sc.

Finish off and weave in ends.

Finishing
Step 1:
Sew Sleeves in armhole openings, easing as necessary.

Step 2:
Sew sleeve and side seams.

Step 3:
Sew buttons opposite buttonholes.

Scalloped Tunic

designed by Melissa Leapman

Sizes:

	Small	Medium	Large
Chest Measurement:	30"-32"	34"-36"	38"-40"
Finished Chest Measurement:	38"	42"	46"

Note: Instructions are written for size small; changes for larger sizes are in parentheses.

Materials:

Spinrite® Lily® Sugar 'n Cream Sport (1.75 oz ball), 16 (17, 19) balls Strawberry Passion #012—or other sport weight yarn worked to gauge

Size F (3.75mm) crochet hook, or size required for gauge

Size E (3.5mm) crochet hook

Size 16 tapestry needle

Gauge:

Note: See "A Word about Gauge" on page 5.

With larger size hook:

13 dc = 3"

7 rows = 3"

In pattern with larger size hook:

6 ch-2 sps = 3¹/₂"

10 rows = 3¹/₂"

All measurements are approximate.

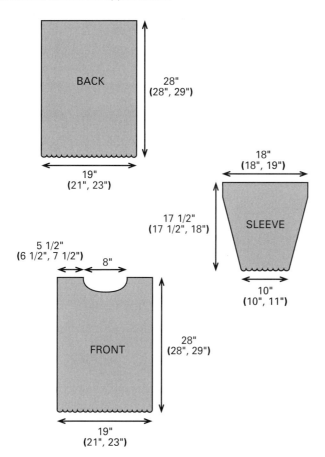

Instructions

Back

With larger size hook, ch 104 (116, 128).

Row 1 (right side):
Sc in 2nd ch from hook; * sk next 2 chs, 5 dc in next ch; sk next 2 chs, sc in next ch; rep from * 16 (18, 20) times more—17 (19, 21) 5-dc groups. Ch 5 (counts as first dc and ch-2 sp on following rows), turn.

Row 2:
Sk first sc and next 2 dc, sc in next dc, ch 2, dc in next sc; * ch 2, sk next 2 dc, sc in next dc, ch 2, dc in next sc; rep from * across. Ch 1, turn.

Row 3:
Sc in first dc, 5 dc in next sc; * sc in next dc, 5 dc in next sc; rep from * to turning ch-5; sk next 2 chs of turning ch, sc in next ch. Ch 5, turn.

Rep Rows 2 and 3 until piece measures 28" (28", 29") from beg, ending by working a wrong side row. Finish off.

Lower Edging:

Hold piece with right side facing you and beg ch at top; make lp on hook and join with an sc in first unused lp of beg ch; working in rem unused lps, * sk next 2 lps, 5 dc in next lp; sk next 2 lps, sc in next lp; rep from * across.

Finish off and weave in all ends.

continued

Color photograph, page 35

Front
Work same as Back until piece measures 8 rows less than back from beg, ending by working a wrong side row.

Left Neck Shaping:
Row 1 (right side):
Sc in first dc; * 5 dc in next sc; sc in next dc; rep from * 4 (5, 6) times more. Ch 3 (counts as first dc on following rows), turn.

Row 2:
Sk first sc and next 2 dc, sc in next dc, ch 2; * dc in next sc, ch 2, sk next 2 dc, sc in next dc, ch 2; rep from * 3 (4, 5) times more; dc in next sc. Ch 1, turn.

Row 3:
Sc in first dc; * 5 dc in next sc; sc in next dc; rep from * 3 (4, 5) times more; 3 dc in next sc. Ch 1, turn, leaving turning ch-3 unworked.

Row 4:
Sc in first dc, ch 2, sk next 2 dc; * dc in next sc, ch 2, sk next 2 dc, sc in next dc, ch 2; rep from * 3 (4, 5) times more; dc in next sc. Ch 1, turn.

Row 5:
Sc in first dc; * 5 dc in next sc; sc in next dc; rep from * 3 (4, 5) times more; 3 dc in next sc. Ch 1, turn.

Rows 6 and 7:
Rep Rows 4 and 5.

Row 8:
Rep Row 4. At end of row, finish off.

Right Neck Shaping:
Hold front with right side facing you; sk next 14 ch-2 sps from left neck shaping, make lp on hook and join with an sc in next dc.

Row 1 (right side):
5 dc in next sc; * sc in next dc, 5 dc in next sc; rep from * 3 (4, 5) times more; sk next 2 chs of turning ch, sc in next ch. Ch 5, turn.

Row 2:
Sk first sc and next 2 dc, sc in next dc; * ch 2, dc in next sc, ch 2, sk next 2 dc, sc in next dc; rep from * 3 (4, 5) times more; sk next 2 dc, dc in joining sc. Ch 1, turn.

Row 3:
Sk first dc, sl st in next sc, ch 3 (counts as a dc on this and following rows), 2 dc in same sc; * sc in next dc, 5 dc in next sc; rep from * 3 (4, 5) times more; sk next 2 chs of turning ch-5, sc in next ch. Ch 5, turn.

Row 4:
Sk first sc and next 2 dc; * sc in next dc, ch 2, dc in next sc, ch 2, sk next 2 dc; rep from * 3 (4, 5) times more; sc in 3rd ch of beg ch-3. Ch 3, turn.

Row 5:
2 dc in first sc; * sc in next dc, 5 dc in next sc; rep from * 3 (4, 5) times more; sk next 2 chs of turning ch-5, sc in next ch. Ch 5, turn.

Row 6:
Sk first sc and next 2 dc; * sc in next dc, ch 2, dc in next sc, ch 2, sk next 2 dc; rep from * 3 (4, 5) times more; sc in 3rd ch of turning ch-3. Ch 3, turn.

Rows 7 and 8:
Rep Rows 5 and 6. At end of Row 8, do not ch 3; do not turn. Finish off.

Lower Edging:
Work same as Back Lower Edging.

Sleeve (make 2)
With larger size hook, ch 56 (56, 62).

Row 1 (right side):
Sc in 2nd ch from hook; * sk next 2 chs, 5 dc in next ch; sk next 2 chs, sc in next ch; rep from * 8 (8, 9) times more—9 (9, 10) 5-dc groups. Ch 5 (counts as first dc and ch-2 sp on following rows), turn.

Row 2:
Sk first sc and next 2 dc, sc in next dc, ch 2, dc in next sc; * ch 2, sk next 2 dc, sc in next dc, ch 2, dc in next sc; rep from * across. Ch 1, turn.

Row 3:
Sc in first dc, 5 dc in next sc; * sc in next dc, 5 dc in next sc; rep from * to turning ch-5; sk next 2 chs of turning ch, sc in next ch. Ch 1, turn.

Row 4:
In first sc work (sc, ch 2, dc); ch 2, sk next 2 dc, sc in next dc, ch 2, sk next 2 dc; * dc in next sc, ch 2, sk next 2 dc, sc in next dc, ch 2, sk next 2 dc; rep from * to last sc; in last sc work (dc, ch 2, sc). Ch 3 (counts as first dc on following rows), turn.

Row 5:
2 dc in first sc; sc in next dc; * 5 dc in next sc; sc in next dc; rep from * to last sc; 3 dc in last sc. Ch 1, turn.

Row 6:
Sc in first dc, ch 2, sk next 2 dc, dc in next sc, ch 2, sk next 2 dc; * sc in next dc, ch 2, sk next 2 dc, dc in next sc, ch 2, sk next 2 dc, sc in next dc; rep from * to turning ch-3; sc in 3rd ch of turning ch-3. Ch 3, turn.

Rows 7 and 8:
Rep Rows 5 and 6.

Row 9:
4 dc in first sc; sc in next dc; * 5 dc in next sc; sc in next dc; rep from * to last sc; 5 dc in last sc. Ch 5, turn.

Row 10:
Sk first 2 dc, sc in next dc, ch 2, sk next 2 dc, dc in next sc; * ch 2, sk next 2 dc, sc in next dc, ch 2, sk next 2 dc, dc in next sc; rep from * to last 4 dc and turning ch-3; ch 2, sk next 2 dc, sc in next dc, ch 2, sk next dc, dc in 3rd ch of turning ch-3. Ch 1, turn.

Row 11:
Sc in first dc, 5 dc in next sc; * sc in next dc, 5 dc in next sc; rep from * to turning ch-5; sk next 2 chs of turning ch, sc in next ch. Ch 5, turn.

Row 12:
Sk first sc and next 2 dc, sc in next dc, ch 2, dc in next sc; * ch 2, sk next 2 dc, sc in next dc, ch 2, dc in next sc; rep from * across. Ch 1, turn.

Row 13:
Sc in first dc, 5 dc in next sc; * sc in next dc, 5 dc in next sc; rep from * to turning ch-5; sk next 2 chs of turning ch, sc in next ch. Ch 1, turn.

Rows 14 through 43:
Rep Rows 4 through 13 three times more. At end of Row 43, ch 5, turn.

Row 44:
Rep Row 12.

Row 45:
Rep Row 11.

Rep Rows 44 and 45 until piece measures 17½" (17½", 18") from beg. Finish off.

Lower Border:
Hold sleeve with right side facing you and beg ch at top; make lp on hook and join with an sc in first unused lp of beg ch; working in rem unused lps, * sk next 2 lps, 5 dc in next lp; sk next 2 lps, sc in next lp; rep from * across.

Finish off and weave in all ends. Mark 5-dc group on either side of center seven 5-dc groups on back neck edge.

Sew shoulder seams, beg each shoulder seam with the sc in 3rd dc of each marked group.

Neck Band
With right side facing you and smaller size hook, join yarn in right shoulder seam; ch 3, 4 dc in same sp; working across back neck edge, sc in next dc, (5 dc in next sc, sc in next dc) 8 times; 5 dc in left shoulder seam; working along left front neck edge in sps formed by edge dc and turning chs, (sc in next sp, 5 dc in next sp) twice; working across front neck edge, sc in next dc, (5 dc in next sc, sc in next dc) 7 times; working along right front neck edge in sps formed by edge dc and turning chs, (5 dc in next sp, sc in next sp) twice; join in 3rd ch of beg ch-3.

Finish off and weave in ends.

Finishing
Step 1:
Mark 9" (9", 9½") from each shoulder seam along front and back edge. Sew sleeves between markers.

Step 2:
Sew sleeve and side seams.

Popover in Pastels
designed by Melissa Leapman

Sizes:

	Small	Medium	Large
Chest Measurement:	30"-32"	34"-36"	38"-40"
Finished Chest Measurement:	36"	40"	44"

Note: Instructions are written for size small; changes for larger sizes are in parentheses.

Materials:
Coats and Clark Southmaid Cotton 8 (2.5 oz skein), 6 (7, 8) skeins White #801; 2 (2, 3) skeins Yellow #808; 1 (2, 2) skeins Carnation #817; 2 (2, 2) skeins Periwinkle #810 and Lilac #818; 1 (1, 1) skein Moss Green #814—or other sport weight yarn worked to gauge
Size F (3.75mm) crochet hook, or size required for gauge
Size 16 tapestry needle

Gauge:
Note: See "A Word about Gauge" on page 5.
5 sc = 1"
5 sc rows = 1"
In pattern:
18 sc = 4"
18 rows = 4"

continued

All measurements are approximate.

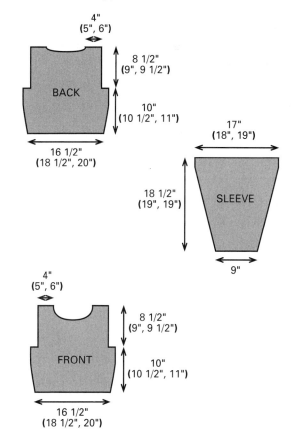

Color photograph, back cover

Pattern Stitches

Long Double Crochet (long dc):
YO, insert hook in sc indicated on 2nd row below, draw up lp to height of working row, (YO, draw through 2 lps on hook) twice—long dc made.
Note: On working row, skip sc behind long dc.

Popcorn (PC):
4 hdc in st indicated; drop lp from hook, insert hook in first hdc made; draw dropped lp through—PC made.

Instructions

Back
With white, ch 76 (84, 92).

Row 1 (right side):
Sc in 2nd ch from hook and in each rem ch—75 (83, 91) sc. Ch 1, turn.

Row 2:
Sc in each sc. Change to yellow by drawing lp through; cut white. Ch 1, turn.

Row 3:
Sc in first 3 sc; * long dc (see Pattern Stitches) in next sc on 2nd row below, sc in next 3 sc; rep from * across. Change to pink by drawing lp through; cut yellow. Ch 1, turn.

Row 4:
Sc in each st. Change to white by drawing lp through; cut pink. Ch 1, turn.

Row 5:
Sc in each sc. Ch 1, turn.

Row 6:
Sc in each sc. Change to blue by drawing lp through; cut white. Ch 1, turn.

Row 7:
Sc in first sc; * ch 1, sk next sc, PC (see Pattern Stitches) in next sc; rep from * to last 2 sc; ch 1, sk next sc, sc in next sc. Change to white by drawing lp through; cut blue. Ch 1, turn.

Row 8:
2 sc in first sc; long dc in next skipped sc on 2nd row below; * sc in next PC, long dc in next skipped sc on 2nd row below; rep from * to last sc; 2 sc in last sc—77 (85, 93) sts.

Row 9:
Sc in each st. Ch 1, turn.

Row 10:
Rep Row 9. At end of row, change to green; cut white. Ch 1, turn.

Row 11:
Sc in first 4 sc; * long dc in next sc on 2nd row below, sc in next 3 sc; rep from * to last sc; sc in last sc. Change to purple; cut green. Ch 1, turn.

Row 12:
Rep Row 9. At end of row, change to white; cut purple. Ch 1, turn.

Rows 13 and 14:
Rep Row 9. At end of Row 14, change to yellow; cut white. Ch 1, turn.

Row 15:
2 sc in first sc; sc in next sc, ch 1, sk next sc; * PC in next sc; ch 1, sk next sc; rep from * to last 2 sc; sc in next sc, 2 sc in next sc—79 (87, 95) sts. Change to white; cut yellow. Ch 1, turn.

Row 16:
Sc in first 3 sc; long dc in next skipped sc on 2nd row below; * sc in next PC, long dc in next skipped sc on 2nd row below; rep from * to last 3 sc; sc in last 3 sc. Ch 1, turn.

Rows 17 and 18:
Rep Row 9. At end of Row 18, change to pink; cut white. Ch 1, turn.

Row 19:
Sc in first sc, long dc in next sc on 2nd row below; * sc in next 3 sc, long dc in next sc on 2nd row below; rep from * to last sc; sc in last sc. Change to blue; cut pink. Ch 1, turn.

Row 20:
Rep Row 9. At end of row, change to white; cut blue. Ch 1, turn.

Row 21:
Rep Row 9.

Row 22:
2 sc in first sc; sc in each sc to last sc; 2 sc in last sc—81 (89, 97) sc. Change to purple; cut white. Ch 1, turn.

Row 23:
Sc in first 2 sc, ch 1, sk next sc; * PC in next sc; ch 1, sk next sc; rep from * to last 2 sc; sc in last 2 sc. Change to white; cut purple. Ch 1, turn.

Row 24:
Sc in first 2 sc, long dc in next skipped sc on 2nd row below; * sc in next PC, long dc in next skipped sc on 2nd row below; rep from * to last 2 sc; sc in last 2 sc. Ch 1, turn.

Rows 25 and 26:
Rep Row 9. At end of Row 26, change to yellow; cut white. Ch 1, turn.

Row 27:
Sc in first 2 sc, long dc in next sc on 2nd row below; * sc in next 3 sc, long dc in next sc on 2nd row below; rep from * to last 2 sc; sc in last 2 sc. Change to pink; cut yellow. Ch 1, turn.

Row 28:
Rep Row 9. At end of row, change to white; cut pink. Ch 1, turn.

Row 29:
2 sc in first sc; sc in each sc to last sc; 2 sc in last sc—83 (91, 99) sc. Ch 1, turn.

Row 30:
Rep Row 9. At end of row change to blue; cut white. Ch 1, turn.

Row 31:
Sc in first sc, ch 1, sk next sc; * PC in next sc; ch 1, sk next sc; rep from * to last sc; sc in last sc. Change to white; cut blue. Ch 1, turn.

Row 32:
Sc in first sc, long dc in next skipped sc on 2nd row below; * sc in next PC, long dc in next skipped sc on 2nd row below; rep from * to last sc; sc in last sc. Ch 1, turn.

Rows 33 and 34:
Rep Row 9. At end of Row 34, change to green; cut white. Ch 1, turn.

Row 35:
Sc in first 3 sc, long dc in next sc on 2nd row below; * sc in next 3 sc, long dc in next sc on 2nd row below; rep from * to last 3 sc; sc in last 3 sc. Change to purple; cut green. Ch 1, turn.

Row 36:
Rep Row 9. At end of row, change to white; cut purple. Ch 1, turn.

Rows 37 and 38:
Rep Row 9. At end of Row 38, change to yellow; cut white. Ch 1, turn.

Row 39:
Sc in first sc, ch 1, sk next sc; * PC in next sc; ch 1, sk next sc; rep from * to last sc; sc in last sc. Change to white; cut yellow. Ch 1, turn.

Row 40:
Sc in first sc, long dc in next skipped sc on 2nd row below; * sc in next PC, long dc in next skipped sc on 2nd row below; rep from * to last sc; sc in last sc. Ch 1, turn.

Rows 41 and 42:
Rep Row 9. At end of Row 42, change to pink; cut white. Ch 1, turn.

Row 43:
Sc in first 3 sc, long dc in next sc on 2nd row below; * sc in next 3 sc, long dc in next sc on 2nd row below; rep from * to last 3 sc; sc in last 3 sc. Change to blue; cut pink. Ch 1, turn.

Row 44:
Rep Row 9. At end of row, change to white; cut blue. Ch 1, turn.

Row 45:
Rep Row 9.

For Size Small Only:
Row 46:
Rep Row 9. At end of row, change to purple; cut white. Turn.

Continue with Armhole Shaping on page 18.

For Size Medium Only:
Row 46:
Rep Row 9. At end of row, change to purple; cut white. Ch 1, turn.

Row 47:
Sc in first sc, ch 1, sk next sc; * PC in next sc; ch 1, sk next sc; rep from * to last sc; sc in last sc. Change to white; cut purple. Ch 1, turn.

Row 48:
Sc in first sc, long dc in next skipped sc on 2nd row below; * sc in next PC, long dc in next skipped sc on 2nd row below; rep from * to last sc; sc in last sc. Turn.

Continue with Armhole Shaping on page 18.

continued

17

For Size Large Only:

Row 46:
Rep Row 9. At end of row, change to purple; cut white. Ch 1, turn.

Row 47:
Sc in first sc, ch 1, sk next sc; * PC in next sc; ch 1, sk next sc; rep from * to last sc; sc in last sc. Change to white; cut purple. Ch 1, turn.

Row 48:
Sc in first sc, long dc in next skipped sc on 2nd row below; * sc in next PC, long dc in next skipped sc on 2nd row below; rep from * to last sc; sc in last sc. Ch 1, turn.

Rows 49 and 50:
Rep Row 9. At end of Row 50, change to yellow; cut white. Turn.

Continue with Armhole Shaping.

Armhole Shaping:
Sl st in first 5 sts, ch 1, sc in same st as last sl st made; work in patt as established to last 4 sts—75 (83, 91) sts. Ch 1, turn, leaving rem sts unworked.

Work even in pattern and color sequence as established until armhole measures 7¹/₂" (8", 8¹/₂"), ending by working a wrong side row.

Right Neck Shaping:
Work first 19 (23, 27) sts in patt as established. Ch 1, turn, leaving rem sts unworked.

Work even in pattern and color sequence as established until armhole measures 8¹/₂" (9", 9¹/₂"). Finish off.

Left Neck Shaping:
Hold piece with right side facing you; sk next 37 sts from right neck shaping, join patt color in next st, ch 1, sc in same st; complete row in patt as established—19 (23, 27) sts.

Work even in pattern and color sequence as established until armhole measures 8¹/₂" (9", 9¹/₂").

Finish off and weave in all ends.

Front
Work same as Back until armhole measures 5¹/₂" (6", 6¹/₂"), ending by working a wrong side row.

Left Neck Shaping:

Row 1 (right side):
Work first 28 (32, 36) sts in patt as established. Ch 1, turn, leaving rem sts unworked.

Row 2:
Dec over first 2 sts (to work dec: draw up lp in each of next 2 sts, YO and draw through all 3 lps on hook—dec made); work in patt across. Ch 1, turn.

Row 3:
Work in patt to last 2 sts; dec. Ch 1, turn.

Row 4:
Dec; work in patt across. Ch 1, turn.

Rows 5 through 10:
Rep Rows 3 and 4 three times more. At end of Row 10—19 (23, 27) sts. Ch 1, turn.

Work even in patt until armhole measures same as Back armhole. Finish off.

Right Neck Shaping:
Hold piece with right side facing you; sk next 19 sts from left neck shaping, join patt color in next st.

Row 1 (right side):
Ch 1, sc in same st, work in patt as established across. Ch 1, turn.

Row 2:
Work in patt to last 2 sts; dec over last 2 sts. Ch 1, turn.

Row 3:
Dec; work in patt across. Ch 1, turn.

Row 4:
Work in patt to last 2 sts; dec. Ch 1, turn.

Rows 5 through 10:
Rep Rows 3 and 4 three times more. At end of Row 10—19 (23, 27) sts. Ch 1, turn.

Work even in patt until armhole measures same as Back armhole.

Finish off and weave in all ends.

Sleeve (make 2)

For Sizes Small and Medium Only:
With white, ch 42.

Row 1 (right side):
Sc in 2nd ch from hook and in each rem ch—41 sc. Ch 1, turn.

Row 2:
Sc in each sc. Change to yellow by drawing lp through; cut white. Ch 1, turn.

Row 3:
Sc in first 2 sc, long dc in next sc on 2nd row below; * sc in next 3 sc, long dc in next sc on 2nd row below; rep from * to last 2 sc; sc in last 2 sc. Change to pink; cut yellow. Ch 1, turn.

Row 4:
Sc in each st. Change to white; cut pink. Ch 1, turn.

Row 5:
2 sc in first sc; sc in each sc to last sc; 2 sc in last sc—43 sc. Ch 1, turn.

Row 6:
Sc in each sc. Change to blue; cut white. Ch 1, turn.

Row 7:
Sc in first sc, ch 1, sk next sc; * PC in next sc; ch 1, sk next sc; rep from * to last sc; sc in last sc. Change to white; cut blue. Ch 1, turn.

Row 8:
Sc in first sc, long dc in next skipped sc on 2nd row below; * sc in next PC, long dc in next skipped sc on 2nd row below; rep from * to last sc; sc in last sc. Ch 1, turn.

Row 9:
Rep Row 5. At end of row—45 sc. Ch 1, turn.

Row 10:
Sc in each sc. Change to green; cut white. Ch 1, turn.

Row 11:
Sc in first 4 sc, long dc in next sc on 2nd row below; * sc in next 3 sc, long dc in next sc on 2nd row below; rep from * to last 4 sc; sc in last 4 sc. Change to purple; cut green. Ch 1, turn.

Row 12:
Sc in each st. Change to white; cut purple. Ch 1, turn.

Row 13:
Rep Row 5. At end of row—47 sc. Ch 1, turn.

Row 14:
Sc in each sc. Change to yellow; cut white. Ch 1, turn.

Row 15:
Rep Row 7. At end of row, change to white; cut yellow. Ch 1, turn.

Row 16:
Rep Row 8.

Row 17:
Rep Row 5. At end of row—49 sc. Ch 1, turn.

Row 18:
Sc in each sc. Change to pink; cut white. Ch 1, turn.

Row 19:
Sc in first 2 sc, long dc in next sc on 2nd row below; * sc in next 3 sc, long dc in next sc on 2nd row below; rep from * to last 2 sc; sc in last 2 sc. Change to blue; cut pink. Ch 1, turn.

Row 20:
Sc in each st. Change to white; cut blue. Ch 1, turn.

Row 21:
Rep Row 5. At end of row—51 sc. Ch 1, turn.

Row 22:
Sc in each sc. Change to purple; cut white. Ch 1, turn.

Row 23:
Rep Row 7. At end of row, change to white; cut purple. Ch 1, turn.

Row 24:
Rep Row 8.

Row 25:
2 sc in first sc; sc in each rem sc to last sc; 2 sc in last sc—53 sc. Ch 1, turn.

For Sizes Small and Medium Only:
Continue in pattern and color sequence as established, inc one st each end every 4th row 12 (14) times more—77 (81) sc.

Work even in pattern and color sequence until sleeve measures 18$\frac{1}{2}$" (19") from beg.

Finish off and weave in all ends.

For Size Large Only:
With white, ch 42.

Row 1:
Sc in 2nd ch from hook and in each rem ch—41 sc. Ch 1, turn.

Row 2:
Sc in each sc. Change to yellow by drawing lp through; cut white. Ch 1, turn.

Row 3:
2 sc in first sc; sc in next sc, long dc in next sc on 2nd row below; * sc in next 3 sc, long dc in next sc on 2nd row below; rep from * to last 2 sc; sc in next sc, 2 sc in next sc. Change to pink; cut yellow. Ch 1, turn.

Row 4:
Sc in each st. Change to white; cut pink. Ch 1, turn.

Row 5:
2 sc in first sc; sc in each sc to last sc; 2 sc in last sc—45 sc. Ch 1, turn.

Row 6:
Sc in each sc. Change to blue; cut white. Ch 1, turn.

Row 7:
2 sc in first sc; sc in next sc, ch 1, sk next sc; * PC in next sc; ch 1, sk next sc; rep from * to last 2 sc; sc in next sc, 2 sc in next sc—47 sc. Change to white; cut blue. Ch 1, turn.

Row 8:
Sc in first 3 sc, long dc in next skipped sc on 2nd row below; * sc in next PC, long dc in next skipped sc on 2nd row below; rep from * to last 3 sc; sc in last 3 sc. Ch 1, turn.

Row 9:
Rep Row 5. At end of row—49 sc. Ch 1, turn.

Row 10:
Sc in each sc. Change to green; cut white. Ch 1, turn.

continued

19

Row 11:
Rep Row 3. At end of row—51 sc. Change to purple; cut green. Ch 1, turn.

Row 12:
Sc in each st. Change to white; cut purple. Ch 1, turn.

Row 13:
Rep Row 5. At end of row—53 sc. Ch 1, turn.

Row 14:
Sc in each sc. Change to yellow; cut white. Ch 1, turn.

Row 15:
Rep Row 7. At end of row—55 sc. Change to white; cut yellow. Ch 1, turn.

Row 16:
Rep Row 8.

Row 17:
Rep Row 5. At end of row—57 sc. Ch 1, turn.

Row 18:
Sc in each sc. Change to pink; cut white. Ch 1, turn.

Row 19:
Sc in first 2 sc, long dc in next sc on 2nd row below; * sc in next 3 sc, long dc in next sc on 2nd row below; rep from * to last 2 sc; sc in last 2 sc. Change to blue; cut pink. Ch 1, turn.

Row 20:
Sc in each st. Change to white; cut blue. Ch 1, turn.

Row 21:
Rep Row 5. At end of row—59 sc. Ch 1, turn.

Row 22:
Sc in each sc. Change to purple; cut white. Ch 1, turn.

Row 23:
Sc in first sc, ch 1, sk next sc; * PC in next sc; ch 1, sk next sc; rep from * to last sc; sc in last sc. Change to white; cut purple. Ch 1, turn.

Row 24:
Sc in first sc, long dc in next skipped sc on 2nd row below; * sc in next PC, long dc in next skipped sc on 2nd row below; rep from * to last sc; sc in last sc. Ch 1, turn.

Row 25:
2 sc in first sc; sc in each rem sc to last sc; 2 sc in last sc— 61 sc. Ch 1, turn.

Continue in pattern and color sequence as established, inc one st each end every 4th row 12 times more—85 sc.

Work even in pattern and color sequence until sleeve measures 19" from beg.

Finish off and weave in all ends.

Sew shoulder seams.

Neck Band
Hold sweater with right side facing you and right shoulder at top; with white, make lp on hook and join with an sc in right shoulder seam.

Rnd 1:
Working along right back neck edge, sc in side of each row; working across back neck edge, sc in each sc; working along left back neck edge, sc in side of each row, sc in left shoulder seam; working along left front neck edge, sc in side of each row; working across front neck edge, sc in each sc; working along right front neck edge, sc in side of each row; join in joining sc.

Rnd 2:
Ch 1, sc in same sc and in each rem sc; join in first sc.

Finish off and weave in ends.

Finishing
Step 1:
Referring to diagram , sew Sleeves in armhole openings between A and B, having center of Sleeves at shoulder seams.

Step 2:
Beginning at B, sew sleeve seams matching corresponding rows. Sew side seams, matching corresponding rows.

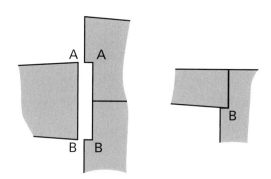

Lace-edged Crop Top

designed by Melissa Leapman

Sizes:

	Small	Medium	Large
Chest Measurement:	30"-32"	34"-36"	38"-40"
Finished Chest Measurement:	34"	38"	42"

Note: Instructions are written for size small; changes for larger sizes are in parentheses.

Materials:

Spinrite® Lily® Sugar 'n Cream Sport (1.75 oz ball), 12 (12, 13) balls French Rose #20—or other sport weight yarn worked to gauge
Size F (3.75mm) crochet hook, or size required for gauge
Size E (3.5mm) crochet hook
Size 16 tapestry needle

Gauge:

Note: See "A Word about Gauge" on page 5.
With larger size hook:
9 dc = 2"
2 dc rows = 1"
In pattern with larger size hook:
(FPdc, V-st, FPdc) = 1"
3 rows = 1"

All measurements are approximate.

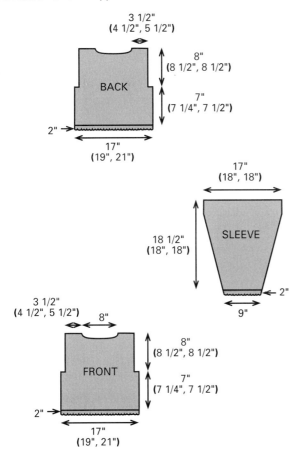

Pattern Stitches

Back Post Double Crochet (BPdc):

YO, insert hook from back to front to back around post (see Stitch Guide on page 5) of st indicated, draw up lp, (YO, draw through 2 lps on hook) twice—BPdc made.

Front Post Double Crochet (FPdc):

YO, insert hook from front to back to front around post (see Stitch Guide on page 5) of st indicated, draw up lp, (YO, draw through 2 lps on hook) twice—FPdc made.

Cluster (CL):

Keeping last lp of each dc on hook, 3 dc in st indicated; YO and draw through all 4 lps on hook—CL made.

2-Double Crochet Cluster (2-dc CL):

Keeping last lp of each dc on hook, 2 dc in st indicated; YO and draw through all 3 lps on hook—2-dc CL made.

Instructions

Back

With larger size hook, ch 91 (99, 107).

continued

Color photograph, back cover

Row 1 (right side):
In 5th ch from hook work (dc, ch 1, dc)—V-st made; * sk next ch, dc in next ch, sk next ch, in next ch work (dc, ch 1, dc)—V-st made; rep from * 20 (22, 24) times more; sk next ch, dc in next ch—22 (24, 26) V-sts. Ch 2 (counts as first hdc on following rows), turn.

Row 2:
* V-st in ch-1 sp of next V-st; sk next dc of same V-st, BPdc (see Pattern Stitches on page 21) around next dc; rep from * 20 (22, 24) times more; V-st in ch-1 sp of next V-st; hdc in 4th ch of beg 4 skipped chs. Ch 2, turn.

Row 3:
V-st in next V-st; * FPdc (see Pattern Stitches on page 21) around next BPdc; V-st in next V-st; rep from * 20 (22, 24) times more; hdc in 2nd ch of turning ch-2. Ch 2, turn.

Row 4:
V-st in next V-st; * BPdc around next FPdc, V-st in next V-st; rep from * 20 (22, 24) times more; hdc in 2nd ch of turning ch-2. Ch 2, turn.

Rep Rows 3 and 4 until piece measures 7" (7¼", 7½") from beg, ending by working a wrong side row. At end of last row, do not ch 2. Ch 1, turn.

Armhole Shaping:
Row 1 (right side):
Sl st in first 2 dc, in next ch-1 sp, and in next 2 dc; ch 2 (counts as an hdc), V-st in next V-st; * FPdc around next BPdc, V-st in next V-st; rep from * 18 (20, 22) times more; hdc in next BPdc. Ch 2, turn, leaving rem sts unworked.

Row 2:
V-st in next V-st; * BPdc around next FPdc, V-st in next V-st; rep from * 18 (20, 22) times more; hdc in 2nd ch of turning ch-2. Ch 2, turn.

Row 3:
V-st in next V-st; * FPdc around next BPdc, V-st in next V-st; rep from * 18 (20, 22) times more; hdc in 2nd ch of turning ch-2. Ch 2, turn.

Rep Rows 2 and 3 until armhole measures 7½" (8", 8"), ending by working a wrong side row.

Right Neck Shaping:
Row 1 (right side):
V-st in next V-st; * FPdc around next BPdc, V-st in next V-st; rep from * 3 (4, 5) times more; hdc in next BPdc— 5 (6, 7) V-sts. Ch 2, turn.

Row 2:
V-st in next V-st; * BPdc around next FPdc, V-st in next V-st; rep from * 3 (4, 5) times more; hdc in 2nd ch of turning ch-2. Finish off.

Left Neck Shaping:
Hold Back with right side facing you; sk next 10 V-sts from right neck shaping, join yarn in next FPdc.

Row 1 (right side):
Ch 2, V-st in next V-st; * FPdc around next BPdc, V-st in next V-st; rep from * 3 (4, 5) times more; hdc in 2nd ch of turning ch-2. Ch 2, turn.

Row 2:
V-st in next V-st; * BPdc around next FPdc, V-st in next V-st; rep from * 3 (4, 5) times more; hdc in 2nd ch of beg ch-2. Finish off.

Lower Back Edging:
Hold Back with right side facing you and beg ch at top. With smaller size hook, make lp on hook and join with an sc in first unused lp of beg ch.

Row 1 (right side):
Working in rem unused lps and skipped chs of beg ch, sc in each lp and in each ch—89 (97, 105) sc. Ch 1, turn.

Row 2:
Sc in each sc. Ch 1, turn.

Row 3:
Sc in first sc; * ch 5, sk next 3 sc, sc in next sc; rep from * across—22 (24, 26) ch-5 sps. Ch 3 (counts as first dc on following rows), turn.

Row 4:
Dc in first sc; * ch 1, sc in next ch-5 sp, ch 1, CL (see Pattern Stitches on page 21) in next sc; rep from * 20 (22, 24) times more; ch 1, sc in next ch-5 sp, ch 1, 2-dc CL (see Pattern Stitches on page 21) in next sc. Ch 5 (counts as first dc and ch-2 sp on following row), turn.

Row 5:
Sc in next ch-1 sp, sk next sc, sc in next ch-1 sp; * ch 5, sk next CL, sc in next ch-1 sp, sk next sc, sc in next ch-1 sp; rep from * 20 (22, 24) times more; ch 2, sk next dc, dc in 3rd ch of turning ch-3. Ch 1, turn.

Row 6:
Sc in first dc, ch 4; * sc in next ch-5 sp, ch 4; rep from * 20 (22, 24) times more; sk next 2 chs, sc in next ch. Ch 1, turn.

Row 7:
Sc in first sc; * in next ch-4 sp work (2 sc, ch 3, sl st in 3rd ch from hook, 2 sc); rep from * 21 (23, 25) times more; sc in next sc.

Finish off and weave in all ends.

Front
Work same as Back until armhole measures 5½" (6¼", 6¼"), ending by working a wrong side row.

Left Neck and Shoulder Shaping:

Row 1 (right side):
* V-st in next V-st; FPdc around next BPdc; rep from * 5 (6, 7) times more; hdc in ch-1 sp of next V-st. Ch 2, turn, leaving rem sts unworked.

Row 2:
* BPdc around next FPdc, V-st in next V-st; rep from * 5 (6, 7) times more; hdc in 2nd ch of turning ch-2. Ch 2, turn.

Row 3:
* V-st in next V-st; FPdc around next BPdc; rep from * 4 (5, 6) times more; hdc in ch-1 sp of next V-st. Ch 2, turn, leaving rem sts unworked.

Row 4:
* BPdc around next FPdc, V-st in next V-st; rep from * 4 (5, 6) times more; hdc in 2nd ch of turning ch-2. Ch 2, turn.

Row 5:
* V-st in next V-st; FPdc around next BPdc; rep from * 3 (4, 5) times more; V-st in next V-st; hdc in next BPdc. Ch 2, turn, leaving turning ch unworked.

Row 6:
V-st in next V-st; * BPdc around next FPdc, V-st in next V-st; rep from * 3 (4, 5) times more; hdc in 2nd ch of turning ch-2. Ch 2, turn.

Row 7:
V-st in next V-st; * FPdc around next BPdc, V-st in next V-st; rep from * 3 (4, 5) times more; hdc in 2nd ch of turning ch-2. Ch 2, turn.

Rep Rows 6 and 7 until left front has same number of rows as Back to shoulder. Finish off.

Right Neck and Shoulder Shaping:

Hold Front with right side facing you; sk next 6 V-sts from left neck; join in ch-1 sp of next V-st.

Row 1 (right side):
Ch 2 (counts as an hdc on this and following rows); * FPdc around next BPdc, V-st in next V-st; rep from * 5 (6, 7) times more; hdc in 2nd ch of turning ch-2. Ch 2, turn.

Row 2:
* V-st in next V-st; BPdc around next FPdc; rep from * 5 (6, 7) times more; hdc in 2nd ch of beg ch-2. Ch 1, turn.

Row 3:
Sl st in first hdc, in next 2 dc, and in ch-1 sp of next V-st; ch 2; * FPdc around next BPdc, V-st in next V-st; rep from * 4 (5, 6) times more; hdc in 2nd ch of turning ch-2. Ch 2, turn.

Row 4:
* V-st in next V-st; BPdc around next FPdc; rep from * 4 (5, 6) times more; hdc in 2nd ch of beg ch-2. Ch 1, turn.

Row 5:
Sl st in first hdc and in next BPdc, ch 2, V-st in next V-st; * FPdc around next BPdc, V-st in next V-st; rep from * 3 (4, 5) times more; hdc in 2nd ch of turning ch-2. Ch 2, turn.

Row 6:
V-st in next V-st; * BPdc around next FPdc, V-st in next V-st; rep from * 3 (4, 5) times more; hdc in 2nd ch of beg ch-2. Ch 2, turn.

Row 7:
V-st in next V-st; * FPdc around next BPdc, V-st in next V-st; rep from * 3 (4, 5) times more; hdc in 2nd ch of turning ch-2. Ch 2, turn.

Row 8:
V-st in next V-st; * BPdc around next FPdc, V-st in next V-st; rep from * 3 (4, 5) times more; hdc in 2nd ch of turning ch-2. Ch 2, turn.

Rep Rows 7 and 8 until right front has same number of rows as Back to shoulder. Finish off.

Lower Front Edging:

Hold Front with right side facing you and beg ch at top; with smaller size hook, make lp on hook and join with an sc in first unused lp of beg ch.

Rows 1 through 7:

Rep Rows 1 through 7 of Lower Back Edging.

Sleeve (make 2)

With larger size hook, ch 47.

Row 1 (right side):
In 5th ch from hook work (dc, ch 1, dc)—V-st made; * sk next ch, dc in next ch, sk next ch, in next ch work (dc, ch 1, dc)—V-st made; rep from * 9 times more; sk next ch, dc in next ch—11 V-sts. Ch 2 (counts as first hdc on following rows), turn.

Row 2:
* V-st in ch-1 sp of next V-st; sk next dc of same V-st, BPdc around next dc; rep from * 9 times more; V-st in ch-1 sp of next V-st; hdc in 4th ch of beg 4 skipped chs. Ch 3 (counts as an hdc and a ch-1 sp on following rows), turn.

Row 3:
2 dc in first hdc; V-st in next V-st; * FPdc around next BPdc, V-st in next V-st; rep from * to turning ch-2; in 2nd ch of turning ch-2 work (2 dc, ch 1, hdc). Ch 2, turn.

Row 4:
V-st in next ch-1 sp; sk next dc, BPdc around next dc, V-st in next V-st; * BPdc around next FPdc, V-st in next V-st; rep from * to last 2 dc and turning ch-4; BPdc around next dc, sk next dc, V-st in next ch of turning ch-3, hdc next ch. Ch 2, turn.

continued

Row 5:
V-st in next V-st; * FPdc around next BPdc, V-st in next V-st; rep from * to turning ch-2; hdc in 2nd ch of turning ch-2. Ch 2, turn.

Row 6:
V-st in next V-st; * BPdc around next FPdc, V-st in next V-st; rep from * to turning ch-2; hdc in 2nd ch of turning ch-2. Ch 2, turn.

Row 7:
Rep Row 5.

Row 8:
V-st in next V-st; * BPdc around next FPdc, V-st in next V-st; rep from * to turning ch-2; hdc in 2nd ch of turning ch-2. Ch 3, turn.

Rows 9 through 32 (38, 38):
Rep Rows 3 through 8, 4 (5, 5) times more. At end of Row 32 (38, 38)—21 (23, 23) V-sts. At end of same row, do not ch 3. Ch 2, turn.

Rep Rows 5 and 6 until sleeve measures 18½" (18", 18") from beg. Finish off.

Sleeve Edging:
Hold Sleeve with right side facing you and beg ch at top; with smaller size hook, make lp on hook and join with an sc in first unused lp of beg ch.

Row 1 (right side):
Working in rem unused lps of beg ch and skipped chs, sc in each lp and in each ch—45 sc. Ch 1, turn.

Row 2:
Sc in each sc. Ch 1, turn.

Row 3:
Sc in first sc; * ch 5, sk next 3 sc, sc in next sc; rep from * across—11 ch-5 sps. Ch 2 (counts as first dc on following rows), turn.

Row 4:
Dc in first sc; * ch 1, sc in next ch-5 sp, ch 1, CL (see Pattern Stitches on page 21) in next sc; rep from * 9 times more; ch 1, sc in next ch-5 sp, ch 1, 2-dc CL (see Pattern Stitches on page 21) in next sc—10 CLs and one 2-dc CL. Ch 5 (counts as first dc and ch-2 sp on following row), turn.

Row 5:
Sc in next ch-1 sp, sk next sc, sc in next ch-1 sp; * ch 5, sk next CL, sc in next ch-1 sp, sk next sc, sc in next ch-1 sp; rep from * 9 times more; ch 2, sk next dc, dc in 3rd ch of turning ch-3—10 ch-5 sps. Ch 1, turn.

Row 6:
Sc in first dc, ch 4; * sc in next ch-5 sp, ch 4; rep from * 9 times more; sk next 2 chs of turning ch-5, sc in next ch. Ch 1, turn.

Row 7:
Sc in first sc; * in next ch-4 sp work (2 sc, ch 3, sl st in 3rd ch from hook, 2 sc); rep from * 10 times more; sc in next sc.

Finish off and weave in all ends.

Sew shoulder seams carefully matching corresponding sts of Front and Back.

Neck Band
Hold sweater with right side facing you and right shoulder seam at top. With smaller size hook, make lp on hook and join with an sc in right shoulder seam.

Rnd 1 (right side):
Working along right back edge in sps formed by edge sts, 2 sc in next sp; sc in next sp; working across back neck edge, sc in next 31 dc; working along left back edge in sps formed by edge sts, sc in next sp, 2 sc in next sp; 2 sc in left shoulder seam; working along left front neck edge in sps formed by edge sts, (2 sc in next sp, sc in next sp) 4 times; working across front neck edge, sc in next 23 dc; working along right front neck edge in sps formed by edge sts, (sc in next sp, 2 sc in next sp) 4 times; join in joining sc—87 sc.

Rnd 2:
Ch 1, sc in same sc and in each rem sc; join in first sc.

Rnd 3:
Ch 1, sc in same sc and in next 2 sc; ch 3, sl st in 3rd ch from hook; * sc in next 3 sc, ch 3, sl st in 3rd ch from hook; rep from * around; join in first sc.

Finish off and weave in ends.

Finishing
Step 1:
Referring to diagram, sew Sleeves in armhole openings between A and B, having center of Sleeves at shoulder seams.

Step 2:
Beginning at B, sew sleeve seams. Sew side seams.

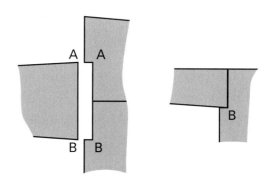

Cool Topper
designed by Hélène Rush

Sizes:

	Small	Medium	Large
Chest Measurement:	34"-36"	38"-40"	42"-44"
Finished Chest Measurement:	39"	43"	47"

Note: Instructions are written for size small; changes for larger sizes are in parentheses.

Materials:

Lion Brand Micro Spun (2.5 oz skein), 7 (8, 9) skeins Lilac #144—or other sport weight yarn worked to gauge
Size H (5mm) crochet hook, or size required for gauge
Size 16 tapestry needle
Four ⅝" gold-tone buttons
Sewing needle and matching thread

Gauge:

Note: See "A Word about Gauge" on page 5.
18 hdc = 4"
15 hdc rows = 4"

All measurements are approximate.

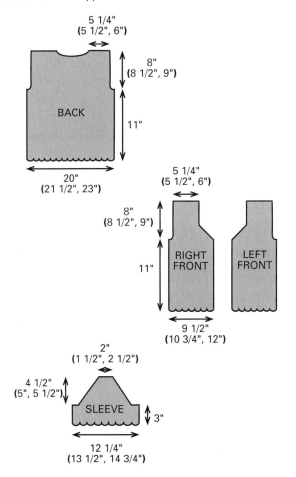

Instructions

Back

Lower Section (worked from underarm to lower edge):
Ch 92 (98, 104).

Row 1 (right side):
Sc in 2nd ch from hook; * sk next 2 chs, 5 dc in next ch; sk next 2 chs, sc in next ch; rep from * 14 (15, 16) times more—91 (97, 103) sts. Ch 3 (counts as first dc on following rows), turn.

Row 2:
2 dc in first sc; * † sk next 2 dc, sc in next dc, sk next 2 dc †; 5 dc in next sc; rep from * 13 (14, 15) times more, then rep from † to † once; 3 dc in next sc. Ch 1, turn.

Row 3:
Sc in first dc; * † sk next 2 dc, 5 dc in next sc; sk next 2 dc †; sc in next dc; rep from * 13 (14, 15) times more, then rep from † to † once; sc in 3rd ch of turning ch-3. Ch 3, turn.

Rep Rows 2 and 3 until piece measures 11" from beg. Finish off.

Yoke:

Hold lower section with right side facing you and beg ch at top; make lp on hook and join with an sc in first unused lp of beg ch.

continued

Color photograph, back cover

Row 1 (right side):
Working in rem unused lps of beg ch, sc in each lp—
91 (97, 103) sc. Ch 1, turn.

Row 2:
Sl st in first 6 sc, ch 2 (counts as an hdc on following row),
hdc in each sc to last 5 sc—81 (87, 93) hdc. Ch 2 (counts as
first hdc on following row), turn, leaving rem sts unworked.

Row 3:
Sk first 2 hdc, hdc in each rem hdc to beg ch-2—79 (85,
91) hdc. Ch 2, turn, leaving beg ch-2 unworked.

Row 4:
Sk first 2 hdc, hdc in each rem hdc to turning ch-2—77 (83,
89) hdc. Ch 2, turn, leaving turning ch-2 unworked.

Rows 5 through 7:
Rep Row 4. At end of Row 7—71 (77, 83) hdc. Ch 2, turn.

Row 8:
Sk first hdc, hdc in each rem hdc and in 2nd ch of turning
ch-2. Ch 2, turn.

Rep Row 8 until piece measures 7" (7½", 8") from beg of
yoke, ending by working a wrong side row. Ch 2, turn.

Right Shoulder:
Row 1 (right side):
Sk first hdc, hdc in next 24 (25, 27) hdc—25 (26, 28) hdc.
Ch 2, turn, leaving rem sts unworked.

Row 2:
Sk first 2 hdc, hdc in each rem hdc and in 2nd ch of turning ch-2—24 (25, 27) hdc. Ch 2, turn.

Row 3:
Sk first hdc, hdc in each rem hdc and in 2nd ch of turning
ch-2. Ch 2, turn.

Rep Row 3 until piece measures 8" (8½", 9") from beg of
yoke. Finish off.

Left Shoulder:
Hold Back with right side facing you; sk next 21 (25,
27) hdc from Row 1 of right shoulder, join in next hdc.

Row 1 (right side):
Ch 2 (counts as an hdc), hdc in each hdc and in 2nd ch of
turning ch-2—25 (26, 28) hdc. Ch 2, turn.

Row 2:
Sk first hdc, hdc in next 22 (23, 25) hdc, sk next hdc, hdc in
2nd ch of beg ch-2—24 (25, 27) hdc. Ch 2, turn.

Row 3:
Sk first hdc, hdc in each rem hdc and in 2nd ch of turning
ch-2. Ch 2, turn.

Rep Row 3 until piece measures 8" (8½", 9") from beg of
yoke. Finish off.

Left Front

Lower Section (worked from underarm to lower edge):
Ch 44 (50, 56).

Row 1 (right side):
Sc in 2nd ch from hook; * sk next 2 chs, 5 dc in next ch; sk
next 2 chs, sc in next ch; rep from * 6 (7, 8) times more—
43 (49, 55) sts. Ch 3 (counts as first dc on following
rows), turn.

Row 2:
2 dc in first sc; * † sk next 2 dc, sc in next dc, sk next
2 dc †; 5 dc in next sc; rep from * 5 (6, 7) times more,
then rep from † to † once; 3 dc in next sc. Ch 1, turn.

Row 3:
Sc in first dc; * † sk next 2 dc, 5 dc in next sc; sk next
2 dc †; sc in next dc; rep from * 5 (6, 7) times more,
then rep from † to † once; sc in 3rd ch of turning ch-3.
Ch 3, turn.

Rep Rows 2 and 3 until piece measures same as back
lower section. Finish off.

Yoke:
Hold left front lower section with right side facing you and
beg ch at top; make lp on hook and join with an sc in first
unused lp of beg ch.

Row 1 (right side):
Working in rem unused lps of beg ch, sc in each lp—43 (49,
55) sc. Ch 2 (counts as first hdc on following rows), turn.

Row 2:
Sk first 2 sc, hdc in next 36 (42, 48) sc—37 (43, 49) hdc.
Ch 2, turn, leaving rem sts unworked.

Row 3:
Sk first 2 hdc, hdc in each rem hdc to turning ch-2—35 (41,
47) hdc. Ch 2, turn, leaving turning ch unworked.

Rows 4 through 6 (8, 10):
Rep Row 3. At end of Row 6 (8, 10)—29 (31, 33) hdc.

Row 7 (9, 11):
Sk first hdc, hdc in each rem hdc and in 2nd ch of turning
ch-2. Ch 2, turn.

Row 8 (10, 12):
Sk first 2 hdc, hdc in each rem hdc and in 2nd ch of turning ch-2—28 (30, 32) hdc. Ch 2, turn.

Rep last 2 rows, 4 (5, 5) times more— 24 (25, 27) hdc.

Rep Row 7 (9, 11) until Left Front is same length as Back
to shoulder. Finish off.

Right Front

Lower Section:
Work same as lower section of left front.

Yoke:

Hold right front lower section with right side facing you and beg ch at top; make lp on hook and join with an sc in first unused lp of beg ch.

Row 1 (right side):
Working in rem unused lps of beg ch, sc in each lp—43 (49, 55) sc. Ch 1, turn.

Row 2:
Sl st in first 6 sc, ch 2 (counts as an hdc), hdc in next 36 (42, 47) sc—37 (43, 48) hdc. Ch 2, turn, leaving joining sc unworked.

Row 3:
Sk first 2 hdc, hdc in each rem hdc to beg ch-2—35 (41, 47) hdc. Ch 2, turn, leaving beg ch-2 unworked.

Row 4:
Sk first 2 hdc, hdc in each rem hdc to turning ch-2. Ch 2, turn, leaving turning ch-2 unworked.

Rows 5 through 6 (8, 10):
Rep Row 4. At end of Row 6 (8, 10)—29 (31, 33) hdc.

Row 7 (9, 11):
Sk first hdc, hdc in each rem hdc and in 2nd ch of turning ch-2. Ch 2, turn.

Row 8 (10, 12):
Sk first hdc, hdc in each rem hdc to last hdc and turning ch-2; sk last hdc, hdc in 2nd ch of turning ch-2—28 (30, 32) hdc. Ch 2, turn.

Rep last 2 rows, 4 (5, 5) times— 24 (25, 27) hdc.

Rep Row 7 (9, 11) until Right Front is same length as Back to shoulder. Finish off.

Sleeve (make 2)

Lower Section (worked from armhole down):
Ch 56 (62, 68).

Row 1 (right side):
Sc in 2nd ch from hook; * sk next 2 chs, 5 dc in next ch; sk next 2 chs, sc in next ch; rep from * 8 (9, 10) times more—55 (61, 67) sts. Ch 3, turn.

Row 2:
2 dc in first sc; * † sk next 2 dc, sc in next dc, sk next 2 dc †; 5 dc in next sc; rep from * 7 (8, 9) times more, then rep from † to † once; 3 dc in next sc. Ch 1, turn.

Row 3:
Sc in first dc; * † sk next 2 dc, 5 dc in next sc; sk next 2 dc †; sc in next dc; rep from * 7 (8, 9) times more, then rep from † to † once; sc in 3rd ch of turning ch-3. Ch 3, turn.

Rep Rows 2 and 3 until piece measures 3" from beg. Finish off.

Upper Sleeve:

Hold lower section with right side facing you and beg ch at top; make lp on hook and join with an sc in first unused lp of beg ch.

Row 1 (right side):
Working in rem unused lps, sc in each lp—55 (61, 67) sc. Ch 1, turn.

Row 2:
Sl st in first 6 sc, ch 2 (counts as an hdc), hdc in each sc to last 5 sc—45 (51, 57) hdc. Ch 2 (counts as first hdc on following rows), turn, leaving rem 5 sts unworked.

Row 3:
Sk first 2 hdc, hdc in each rem hdc to beg ch-2—43 (49, 55) hdc. Ch 2, turn, leaving beg ch-2 unworked.

Row 4:
Sk first 2 hdc, hdc in each rem hdc to turning ch-2—41 (47, 53) hdc. Ch 2, turn, leaving turning ch unworked.

Rows 5 through 14 (15, 16):
Rep Row 4. At end of Row 14 (15, 16)—21 (23, 27) sts.

Row 15 (16, 17):
Dec over first 3 sts [to work dec: (YO, draw up lp in next st) 3 times, YO and draw through all 7 lps on hook—dec made]; hdc in each st to last 2 hdc and turning ch-2; dec over last 2 dc and 2nd ch of turning ch-2—17 (19, 23) sts. Ch 2, turn.

Rep last row, 2 (3, 3) times more—9 (7, 11) sts.

Finish off and weave in all ends.

Sew shoulder seams.

continued

Front and Neck Band:
Hold sweater with right side facing you and right front edge at top; make lp on hook and join with an sc in sp formed by edge st of last row at lower right edge.

Row 1 (right side):
Working in sps formed by edge sts, sc in each sp along right front; working across back neck edge, sc in each hdc; working in sps formed by edge sts, sc in each sp along left front to lower left front edge. Ch 1, turn.

Row 2:
Sc in each sc. Ch 1, turn.

Mark 4 buttonholes evenly spaced along right front edge, having first buttonhole at beg of neck shaping.

Row 3:
* Sc in each sc to next marker; ch 2—buttonhole made; sk next 2 sc; rep from * 3 times more; sc in each rem sc. Ch 1, turn.

Row 4:
Sc in each sc and in each ch.

Finish off and weave in ends.

Finishing
Step 1:
Sew Sleeves to armhole openings, easing to fit.

Step 2:
Sew sleeve and side seams.

Step 3:
Sew buttons opposite buttonholes.

Cozy Chenille Tunic
designed by Hélène Rush

Sizes:

	Small	Medium	Large
Chest Measurement:	34"-36"	38"-40"	42"-44"
Finished Chest Measurement:	42"	46"	50"

Note: Instructions are written for size small; changes for larger sizes are in parentheses.

Materials:
Honeysuckle Yarns Rayon Chenille (88-yd ball), 22 (24, 26) balls Rose # 9—or other sport weight yarn worked to gauge
Size G (4.25mm) crochet hook, or size required for gauge
Size 16 tapestry needle

Gauge:
Note: See "A Word about Gauge" on page 5.
9 dc = 2"
4 dc rows = 2"
In pattern:
(FPdc, shell, FPdc, shell, FPdc, shell, FPdc) = 3¹/₂"
4 rows = 2"

All measurements are approximate.

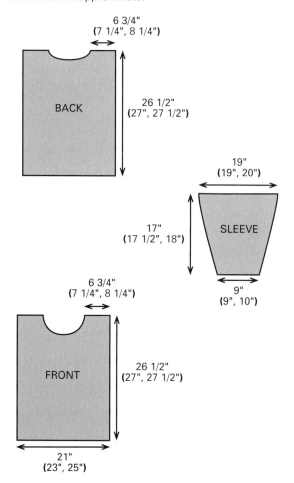

Pattern Stitches

Front Post Double Crochet (FPdc):
YO, insert hook from front to back to front around post (see Stitch Guide on page 5) of st indicated, draw up lp, (YO, draw through 2 lps on hook) twice—FPdc made.

Back Post Double Crochet (BPdc):
YO, insert hook from back to front to back around post (see Stitch Guide on page 5) of st indicated, draw up lp, (YO, draw through 2 lps on hook) twice—BPdc made.

Instructions

Back
Ch 116 (128, 140).

Row 1 (wrong side):
Sc in 2nd ch from hook and in each rem ch—115 (127, 139) sc. Ch 3 (counts as first dc on following rows), turn.

Row 2 (right side):
Sk first 3 sc; * † 5 dc in next sc—shell made; sk next 2 sc, dc in next sc †; sk next 2 sc; rep from * 17 (19, 21) times more, then rep from † to † once—19 (21, 23) shells. Ch 3, turn.

Color photograph, page 33

Row 3:
2 dc in first dc; * † sk next 2 dc, dc in next dc, sk next 2 dc †; shell in next dc; rep from * 17 (19, 21) times more, then rep from † to † once; 3 dc in 3rd ch of turning ch-3—18 (20, 22) shells. Ch 3, turn.

Row 4:
Sk next 2 dc; * † shell in next dc; sk next 2 dc †; dc in next dc, sk next 2 dc; rep from * 17 (19, 21) times more, then rep from † to † once; dc in 3rd ch of turning ch-3—19 (21, 23) shells. Ch 3, turn.

Rows 5 and 6:
Rep Rows 3 and 4.

Row 7:
Rep Row 3.

Row 8:
2 dc in first dc; * † sk next 2 dc, FPdc (see Pattern Stitches) around next dc; sk next 2 dc †; shell in next dc; rep from * 17 (19, 21) times more, then rep from † to † once; 3 dc in 3rd ch of turning ch-3. Ch 3, turn.

Row 9:
2 dc in first dc; * † sk next 2 dc, BPdc (see Pattern Stitches) around next FPdc; sk next 2 dc †; shell in next dc; rep from * 17 (19, 21) times more, then rep from † to † once; 3 dc in 3rd ch of turning ch-3. Ch 3, turn.

Row 10:
2 dc in first dc; * † sk next 2 dc, FPdc around next BPdc, sk next 2 dc †; shell in next dc; rep from * 17 (19, 21) times more, then rep from † to † once; 3 dc in 3rd ch of turning ch-3. Ch 3, turn.

Row 11:
2 dc in first dc; * † sk next 2 dc, BPdc around next FPdc, sk next 2 dc †; shell in next dc; rep from * 17 (19, 21) times more, then rep from † to † once; 3 dc in 3rd ch of turning ch-3. Ch 3, turn.

Rep Rows 10 and 11 until piece measures 26" (26¹/₂", 27"), ending by working a wrong side row.

Right Shoulder Shaping:
FOR SIZE SMALL ONLY:
Row 1 (right side):
2 dc in first dc; * † sk next 2 dc, FPdc around next BPdc, sk next 2 dc †; shell in next dc; rep from * 4 times more, then rep from † to † once; 3 dc in next dc—37 sts. Ch 1, turn, leaving rem sts unworked.

continued

Row 2:
Sc in first dc, hdc in next 2 dc; * BPdc around next FPdc, hdc in next dc, sc in next dc, sk next dc, sc in next dc, hdc in next dc; rep from * 4 times more; BPdc around next FPdc, hdc in next 2 dc, sc in 3rd ch of turning ch-3. Finish off.

FOR SIZES MEDIUM AND LARGE ONLY:
Row 1 (right side):
2 dc in first dc; * sk next 2 dc, FPdc around next BPdc, sk next 2 dc, shell in next dc; rep from * 5 (6) times more; sk next 2 dc, dc in next BPdc—40 (46) sts. Ch 3, turn, leaving rem sts unworked.

Row 2:
* Hdc in next dc, sc in next dc, sk next dc, sc in next dc, hdc in next dc, BPdc around next FPdc; rep from * 5 (6) times more; hdc in next dc, sc in next dc, and in 3rd ch of turning ch-3. Finish off.

Left Shoulder Shaping:
FOR SIZE SMALL ONLY:
Hold Back with right side facing you; sk next 41 dc from right shoulder, join in next dc.

Row 1 (right side):
Ch 3 (counts as a dc), 2 dc in same st as joining; sk next 2 dc; * † FPdc around next BPdc, sk next 2 dc †; shell in next dc; sk next 2 dc; rep from * 4 times more, then rep from † to † once; 3 dc in 3rd ch of turning ch-3—37 sts. Ch 1, turn.

Row 2:
Sc in first 2 dc, hdc in next dc; * BPdc around next FPdc, hdc in next dc, sc in next dc, sk next dc, sc in next dc, hdc in next dc; rep from * 4 times more; BPdc around next FPdc, hdc in next 2 dc, sc in 3rd ch of turning ch-3. Finish off.

FOR SIZES MEDIUM AND LARGE ONLY:
Hold Back with right side facing you; sk next 47 (47) dc from right shoulder, join in next BPdc.

Row 1 (right side):
Ch 3 (counts as a dc), sk next 2 dc; * shell in next dc; sk next 2 dc, FPdc around next BPdc, sk next 2 dc; rep from * 5 (6) times more; 3 dc in 3rd ch of turning ch-3—40 (46) sts. Ch 1, turn.

Row 2:
Sc in first 2 dc, hdc in next dc; * BPdc around next FPdc, hdc in next dc, sc in next dc, sk next dc, sc in next dc, hdc in next dc; rep from * 5 (6) times more; dc in next BPdc. Finish off.

Front
Work same as for Back until piece measures 24" (24¹/₂", 25") from beg, ending by working a wrong side row.

Left Neck and Shoulder Shaping:
FOR SIZE SMALL ONLY:
Row 1 (right side):
2 dc in first dc; sk next 2 dc; * FPdc around next BPdc, sk next 2 dc, shell in next dc; sk next 2 dc; rep from * 5 times more; dc in next BPdc—40 sts. Ch 3, turn.

Row 2:
Sk next 2 dc, 3 dc in next dc; sk next 2 dc; * † BPdc around next FPdc, sk next 2 dc †; shell in next dc; sk next 2 dc; rep from * 4 (6, 6) times more, then rep from † to † once; 3 dc in 3rd ch of turning ch-3. Ch 3, turn.

Row 3:
2 dc in first dc; sk next 2 dc; * FPdc around next BPdc, sk next 2 dc, shell in next dc; sk next 2 dc; rep from * 4 times more; FPdc around next BPdc, sk next 2 dc, 3 dc in next dc—37 sts. Ch 3, turn, leaving turning ch-3 unworked.

Row 4:
2 dc in first dc; sk next 2 dc; * † BPdc around next FPdc, sk next 2 dc †; shell in next dc; sk next 2 dc; rep from * 4 times more, then rep from † to † once; 3 dc in 3rd ch of turning ch-3. Ch 3, turn.

Row 5:
2 dc in first dc; sk next 2 dc; * † FPdc around next BPdc, sk next 2 dc †; shell in next dc; sk next 2 dc; rep from * 4 times more, then rep from † to † once; 3 dc in next dc. Ch 1, turn.

Row 6:
Sc in first 2 dc, hdc in next dc; * † BPdc around next FPdc, hdc in next dc, sc in next dc †; sk next dc, sc in next dc, hdc in next dc; rep from * 4 times more, then rep from † to † once; sc in 3rd ch of turning ch-3. Finish off.

FOR SIZES MEDIUM AND LARGE ONLY:
Row 1 (right side):
2 dc in first dc; sk next 2 dc; * † FPdc around next BPdc, sk next 2 dc †; shell in next dc; sk next 2 dc; rep from * 5 (6) times more, then rep from † to † once; 3 dc in next dc—43 (49) sts. Ch 3, turn, leaving rem sts unworked.

Row 2:
Sk next 2 dc; * † BPdc around next FPdc, sk next 2 dc †; shell in next dc; sk next 2 dc; rep from * 5 (6) times more, then rep from † to † once; 3 dc in 3rd ch of beg ch-3. Ch 3, turn.

Row 3:
2 dc in first dc; sk next 2 dc; * FPdc around next BPdc, sk next 2 dc, shell in next dc; sk next 2 dc; rep from * 5 (6) times more; dc in next BPdc—40 (46) sts. Ch 3, turn, leaving turning ch-3 unworked.

Row 4:
Sk next 2 dc; * shell in next dc; sk next 2 dc, BPdc around next FPdc, sk next 2 dc; rep from * 5 (6) times more; 3 dc in 3rd ch of turning ch-3. Ch 3, turn.

30

Row 5:
2 dc in first dc; * sk next 2 dc, FPdc around next BPdc, sk next 2 dc, shell in next dc; rep from * 5 (6) times more; sk next 2 dc, dc in 3rd ch of turning ch-3. Ch 3, turn.

Row 6:
* Hdc in next dc, sc in next dc, sk next dc, sc in next dc, hdc in next dc, BPdc around next FPdc; rep from * 5 (6) times more; hdc in next dc, sc in next dc and in 3rd ch of turning ch-3. Finish off.

Right Neck and Shoulder Shaping:
FOR SIZE SMALL ONLY:
Hold Front with right side facing you; sk next 35 dc from left neck shaping, join in next BPdc.

Row 1 (right side):
Ch 3 (counts as a dc), sk next 2 dc; * shell in next dc; sk next 2 dc, FPdc around next BPdc, sk next 2 dc; rep from * 5 times more; 3 dc in 3rd ch of turning ch-3—40 sts. Ch 3, turn.

Row 2:
2 dc in first dc; sk next 2 dc; * † BPdc around next FPdc, sk next 2 dc †; shell in next dc; sk next 2 dc; rep from * 4 times more, then rep from † to † once; 3 dc in next dc; sk next 2 dc, dc in 3rd ch of turning ch-3. Turn.

Row 3:
Sl st in first 2 dc, ch 3 (counts as a dc), 2 dc in same dc as last sl st made; sk next 2 dc; * † FPdc around next BPdc, sk next 2 dc †; shell in next dc; sk next 2 dc; rep from * 4 times more, then rep from † to † once; 3 dc in 3rd ch of turning ch-3—37 sts. Ch 3, turn.

Row 4:
2 dc in first dc; sk next 2 dc; * † BPdc around next FPdc, sk next 2 dc †; shell in next dc; sk next 2 dc; rep from * 4 times more, then rep from † to † once; 3 dc in 3rd ch of turning ch-3. Ch 3, turn.

Row 5:
2 dc in first dc; sk next 2 dc; * † FPdc around next BPdc, sk next 2 dc †; shell in next dc; sk next 2 dc; rep from * 4 times more, then rep from † to † once; 3 dc in 3rd ch of turning ch-3. Ch 1, turn.

Row 6:
Sc in first 2 dc, hdc in next dc; * † BPdc around next FPdc, hdc in next dc, sc in next dc †; sk next dc, sc in next dc, hdc in next dc; rep from * 4 times more, then rep from † to † once; sc in 3rd ch of turning ch-3. Finish off.

FOR SIZES MEDIUM AND LARGE ONLY:
Hold front with right side facing you; sk next 41 (41) dc from left neck shaping; join in next dc.

Row 1 (right side):
Ch 3 (counts as a dc), 2 dc in same dc as joining; sk next 2 dc; * † FPdc around next BPdc, sk next 2 dc †; shell in next dc; sk next 2 dc; rep from * 5 (6) times more, then

rep from † to † once; 3 dc in 3rd ch of turning ch-3—43 (49) dc. Ch 3, turn.

Row 2:
2 dc in first dc; sk next 2 dc; * † BPdc around next FPdc, sk next 2 dc †; shell in next dc; sk next 2 dc; rep from * 5 (6) times more, then rep from † to † once; dc in 3rd ch of turning ch-3. Ch 3, turn.

Row 3:
Sk first BPdc and next 2 dc; * shell in next dc; sk next 2 dc, FPdc around next BPdc, sk next 2 dc; rep from * 5 (6) times more; 3 dc in 3rd ch of turning ch-3. Ch 3, turn.

Row 4:
2 dc in first dc; sk next 2 dc; * BPdc around next FPdc, sk next 2 dc, shell in next dc; sk next 2 dc; rep from * 5 (6) times more; dc in 3rd ch of turning ch-3. Ch 3, turn.

Row 5:
Sk first 3 dc; * shell in next dc; sk next 2 dc, FPdc around next BPdc, sk next 2 dc; rep from * 5 (6) times more; 3 dc in 3rd ch of turning ch-3. Ch 1, turn.

Row 6:
Sc in first 2 dc, hdc in next dc; * BPdc around next FPdc, hdc in next dc, sc in next dc, sk next dc, sc in next dc, hdc in next dc; rep from * 5 (6) times more; dc in 3rd ch of turning ch-3. Finish off.

Sleeve (make 2)
Ch 50 (50, 56).

Row 1 (wrong side):
Sc in 2nd ch from hook and in each rem ch—49(49, 55) sc. Ch 3 (counts as first dc on following rows), turn.

Row 2 (right side):
Sk first 3 sc; * † 5 dc in next sc—shell made; sk next 2 sc, dc in next sc †; sk next 2 sc; rep from * 6 (6, 7) times more, then rep from † to † once. Ch 3, turn.

Row 3:
2 dc in first dc; * † sk next 2 dc, dc in next dc, sk next 2 dc †; shell in next dc; rep from * 6 (6, 7) times more, then rep from † to † once; 3 dc in 3rd ch of turning ch-3. Ch 3, turn.

Row 4:
Sk first 2 sc; * † shell in next dc; sk next 2 dc, dc in next dc †; sk next 2 dc; rep from * 6 (6, 7) times more, then rep from † to † once. Ch 3, turn.

Row 5:
Rep Row 3.

Row 6:
3 dc in first dc; * † sk next 2 dc, FPdc around next dc, sk next 2 dc †; shell in next dc; rep from * 6 (6, 7) times more, then rep from † to † once; 4 dc in 3rd ch of turning ch-3—51 (51, 57) dc. Ch 3, turn.

continued

Row 7:
4 dc in first dc; sk next 3 dc, BPdc around next FPdc; * sk next 2 dc, shell in next dc; sk next 2 dc, BPdc around next FPdc; rep from * to last 3 dc and turning ch-3; sk last 3 dc, 5 dc in 3rd ch of turning ch-3—53 (53, 59) sts. Ch 3, turn.

Row 8:
5 dc in first dc; sk next 4 dc, FPdc around next BPdc; * sk next 2 dc, shell in next dc; sk next 2 dc, FPdc around next BPdc; rep from * to last 4 dc and turning ch-3; sk last 4 dc, 6 dc in 3rd ch of turning ch-3—55 (55, 61) sts. Ch 3, turn.

Row 9:
Sk next 2 dc, shell in next dc; sk next 2 dc; * BPdc around next FPdc, sk next 2 dc, shell in next dc; sk next 2 dc; rep from * to turning ch-3; dc in 3rd ch of turning ch-3. Ch 3, turn.

Row 10:
Dc in first dc, sk next 2 dc, shell in next dc; sk next 2 dc; * FPdc around next BPdc, sk next 2 dc, shell in next dc; sk next 2 dc; rep from * to turning ch-3; 2 dc in 3rd ch of turning ch-3—57 (57, 63) sts. Ch 3, turn.

Row 11:
Dc in first 2 dc, sk next 2 dc, shell in next dc; sk next 2 dc; * BPdc around next FPdc, sk next 2 dc, shell in next dc; sk next 2 dc; rep from * to last dc and turning ch-3; dc in last dc, 2 dc in 3rd ch of turning ch-3—59 (59, 65) sts. Ch 3, turn.

Row 12:
2 dc in first dc; dc next dc, FPdc around next dc, sk next 2 dc, shell in next dc; sk next 2 dc; * FPdc around next BPdc, sk next 2 dc, shell in next dc; sk next 2 dc; rep from * to last 2 dc and turning ch-3; FPdc around next dc, dc in next dc, 3 dc in 3rd ch of turning ch-3—63 (63, 69) sts. Ch 3, turn.

Rows 13 through 30:
Rep Rows 7 through 12 three times more. At end of Row 30—99 (99, 105) dc.

Rows 31 and 32:
Rep Rows 7 and 8. At end of Row 32—103 (103, 109) dc.

Row 33:
Sk next 2 dc, shell in next dc; sk next 2 dc; * BPdc around next FPdc, sk next 2 dc, shell in next dc; sk next 2 dc; rep from * to turning ch-3; dc in 3rd ch of turning ch-3. Ch 3, turn.

Row 34:
Sk next 2 dc, shell in next dc; sk next 2 dc; * FPdc around next BPdc, sk next 2 dc, shell in next dc; sk next 2 dc; rep from * to turning ch-3; dc in 3rd ch of turning ch-3. Ch 3, turn.

Rep Rows 33 and 34 until Sleeve measures 17" (17½", 18") from beg. At end of last row, do not ch 3. Ch 2 (counts as first hdc on following row), turn.

Next Row:
Hdc in next dc, sc in next dc, sk next dc, sc in next dc, hdc in next dc; * BPdc around next FPdc, hdc in next dc, sc in next dc, sk next dc, sc in next dc, hdc in next dc; rep from * to turning ch-3; dc in 3rd ch of turning ch-3.

Finish off and weave in all ends.

Sew shoulder seams.

Neck Trim:
Hold tunic with right side of back facing you; make lp on hook and join with an sc in right shoulder seam.

Rnd 1:
Working along right neck edge in sps formed by edge dc and turning chs, 2 sc in each of next 2 sps; working across back neck edge, sc in next 41 (47, 47) sts; working along left neck edge in sps formed by edge dc and turning chs, 2 sc in each of next 2 sps; sc in left shoulder seam; working along left front neck edge in sps formed by edge dc and turning chs, 2 sc in each sp; working across front neck edge, sc in next 35 (41, 41) sts; working along right front neck edge in sps formed by edge dc and turning chs, 2 sc in each sp; join in joining sc.

Rnd 2:
Ch 1, sc in same sc and in each rem sc; join in first sc.

Finish off and weave in ends.

Finishing
Step 1:
Measure 9½" (9½", 10") on each side of shoulder seam and place markers on armhole edge. Sew Sleeves between markers, easing as necessary.

Step 2:
Sew sleeve and side seams, leaving first six rows of front and back open at lower edge.

Cozy Chenille Tunic

Shells and Mesh
Sweater

33

Career Cardigan

34

Scalloped Tunic

Summertime Tee

Mesa Steps Pullover

Mesa Steps Pullover

designed by Sandy Scoville

Sizes:

	Small	Medium	Large
Chest Measurement:	30"-32"	34"-36"	38"-40"
Finished Chest Measurement:	38"	42"	46"

Note: Instructions are written for size small; changes for other sizes are in parentheses.

Materials:

Taki Imports Cotton Classic (1.75 oz skein), 7 (8, 9) skeins each, Ivory #3003 and Adobe #3358—or other sport weight yarn worked to gauge
Size H (5mm) crochet hook, or size required for gauge
Size J (6mm) crochet hook (for joining chain)
Size 16 tapestry needle

Gauge:

Note: See "A Word about Gauge" on page 5.
With smaller size hook:
15 hdc = 4"
3 hdc rows = 1"

All measurements are approximate.

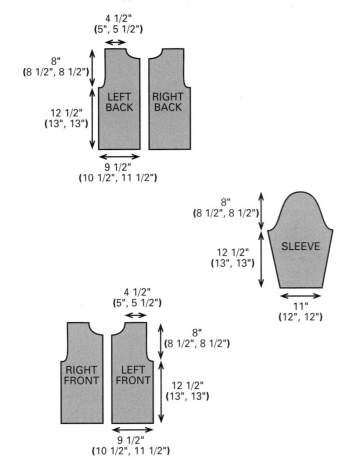

Instructions

Left Front

With smaller size hook and rust, ch 37 (41, 45).

Row 1 (right side):
Hdc in 3rd ch from hook (2 skipped chs count as an hdc) and in each rem ch—36 (40, 44) hdc. Ch 2 (counts as first hdc on following rows), turn.

Row 2:
Sk first hdc, hdc in each rem hdc and in 2nd ch of beg 2 skipped chs. Ch 2, turn.

Row 3:
Sk first hdc, hdc in each rem hdc and in 2nd ch of turning ch-2. Ch 2, turn.

Rows 4 through 6:
Rep Row 3.

Note: When changing colors on following rows, always bring new color under old color; keep unused color on wrong side of work.

Row 7:
Sk first hdc, hdc in next 25 (29, 33) hdc; change to off white by drawing lp through; hdc in next 9 hdc and in 2nd ch of turning ch-2. Ch 2, turn.

continued

Color photograph, page 36

Row 8:
Sk first hdc, hdc in next 9 hdc; change to rust by drawing lp through; hdc in each rem hdc and in 2nd ch of turning ch-2. Ch 2, turn.

Rows 9 through 12:
Rep Rows 7 and 8 twice more.

Note: When unused color is carried across several unworked sts, work over yarn at same time as sts to prevent long loops on the wrong side.

Row 13:
Sk first hdc, hdc in next 15 (19, 23) hdc; bring off white loosely across unworked rust hdc, change to off white; working over off white, hdc in next 19 hdc and in 2nd ch of turning ch-2. Ch 2, turn.

Row 14:
Sk first hdc, hdc in next 19 hdc; change to rust; hdc in each rem hdc and in 2nd ch of turning ch-2. Ch 2, turn.

Row 15:
Sk first hdc, hdc in next 15 (19, 23) hdc; change to off white; hdc in each rem hdc and in 2nd ch of turning ch-2. Ch 2, turn.

Rows 16 and 17:
Rep Rows 14 and 15.

Row 18:
Rep Row 14.

Row 19:
Sk first hdc, hdc in next 5 (9, 13) hdc; bring off white loosely across unworked rust hdc, change to off white; working over off white, hdc in next 29 hdc and in 2nd ch of turning ch-2. Ch 2, turn.

Row 20:
Sk first hdc, hdc in next 29 hdc; change to rust; hdc in each rem hdc and in 2nd ch of turning ch-2. Ch 2, turn.

Row 21:
Sk first hdc, hdc in next 5 (9, 13) hdc; change to off white; hdc in each rem hdc and in 2nd ch of turning ch-2. Ch 2, turn.

Rows 22 and 23:
Rep Rows 20 and 21.

Row 24:
Rep Row 20.

Row 25:
Sk first hdc, hdc in next 5 (9, 13) hdc; continuing with rust and working over off white, hdc in next 10 hdc; change to off white; hdc in next 19 hdc and in 2nd ch of turning ch-2. Ch 2, turn.

Row 26:
Sk first hdc, hdc in next 19 hdc; change to rust; hdc in each rem hdc and in 2nd ch of turning ch-2. Ch 2, turn.

Row 27:
Sk first hdc, hdc in next 15 (19, 23) hdc; change to off white; hdc in each rem hdc and in 2nd ch of turning ch-2. Ch 2, turn.

Rows 28 and 29:
Rep Rows 26 and 27.

Row 30:
Rep Row 26.

Row 31:
Sk first hdc, hdc in next 15 (19, 23) hdc, continuing with rust and working over off white, hdc in next 10 hdc; change to off white; hdc in next 9 hdc and in 2nd ch of turning ch-2. Ch 2, turn.

Row 32:
Sk first hdc, hdc in next 9 hdc; change to rust; hdc in each rem hdc and in 2nd ch of turning ch-2. Ch 2, turn.

Row 33:
Sk first hdc, hdc in next 25 (29, 33) hdc; change to off white; hdc in each rem hdc and in 2nd ch of turning ch-2. Ch 2, turn.

Rows 34 and 35:
Rep Rows 32 and 33.

Row 36:
Rep Row 32. At end of row, cut off white.

Row 37:
Sk first hdc, hdc in each rem hdc and in 2nd ch of turning ch-2. Ch 2, turn.

FOR SIZE SMALL ONLY:
Row 38:
Sk first hdc, hdc in each rem hdc and in 2nd ch of turning ch-2. Ch 1, turn.

Continue with Armhole Shaping below.

FOR SIZES MEDIUM AND LARGE ONLY:
Rows 38 and 39:
Rep Row 37.

Row 40:
Sk first hdc, hdc in each rem hdc and in 2nd ch of turning ch-2. Ch 1, turn.

Continue with Armhole Shaping.

Armhole Shaping:
Row 1 (right side):
Sl st in first 6 hdc, ch 2 (counts as an hdc), dec over next 2 hdc [to work dec: (YO, draw up lp in next hdc) twice; YO and draw through all 5 lps on hook—dec made]; hdc in each rem hdc and in 2nd ch of turning ch-2—30 (34, 38) hdc. Ch 2, turn.

Row 2:
Sk first hdc, hdc in each rem hdc and in 2nd ch of beg ch-2. Change to off white. Ch 2, turn.

Row 3:
Sk first hdc, working over rust, hdc in next 9 (3, 7) hdc; change to rust; hdc in next 19 (29, 29) hdc and in 2nd ch of turning ch-2. Ch 2, turn.

Row 4:
Sk first hdc, hdc in next 19 (29, 29) hdc; change to off white; hdc in each rem hdc and in 2nd ch of turning ch-2. Ch 2, turn.

Row 5:
Sk first hdc, hdc in next 9 (3, 7) hdc; change to rust; hdc in each rem hdc and in 2nd ch of turning ch-2. Ch 2, turn.

Rows 6 and 7:
Rep Rows 4 and 5.

Row 8:
Rep Row 4.

Row 9:
Sk first hdc, hdc in next 9 (3, 7) hdc, working over rust, hdc in next 10 hdc; change to rust; hdc in next 9 (19, 19) hdc and in 2nd ch of turning ch-2. Ch 2, turn.

Row 10:
Sk first hdc, hdc in next 9 (19, 19) hdc; change to off white; hdc in each rem hdc and in 2nd ch of turning ch-2. Ch 2, turn.

Row 11:
Sk first hdc, hdc in next 19 (13, 17) hdc; change to rust; hdc in each rem hdc and in 2nd ch of turning ch-2. Ch 2, turn.

Rows 12 and 13:
Rep Rows 10 and 11.

FOR SIZE SMALL ONLY:
Row 14:
Rep Row 10. At end of row, cut rust.

Row 15:
Sk first hdc, hdc in each rem hdc and in 2nd ch of turning ch-2. Ch 2, turn.

Rows 16 through 20:
Rep Row 15.

Continue with Neckline Shaping.

FOR SIZES MEDIUM AND LARGE ONLY:
Row 14:
Rep Row 10.

Row 15:
Sk first hdc, hdc in next 13 (17) hdc; working over rust, hdc in next 10 hdc; change to rust; hdc in next 9 hdc and in 2nd ch of turning ch-2. Ch 2, turn.

Row 16:
Sk first hdc, hdc in next 9 hdc; change to off white; hdc in each rem hdc and in 2nd ch of turning ch-2. Ch 2, turn.

Row 17:
Sk first hdc, hdc in next 23 (27) hdc; change to rust; hdc in each rem hdc and in 2nd ch of turning ch-2. Ch 2, turn.

Rows 18 and 19:
Rep Rows 16 and 17.

Row 20:
Rep Row 16. At end of row, cut rust.

Row 21:
Sk first hdc, hdc in each rem hdc and in 2nd ch of turning ch-2. Ch 2, turn.

Row 22:
Rep Row 21.

Continue with Neckline Shaping.

Neckline Shaping:
Row 1 (right side):
Sk first hdc, hdc in next 17 (19, 21) hdc—18 (20, 22) hdc. Ch 2, turn, leaving rem hdc unworked.

Row 2:
Sk first hdc, dec; hdc in each rem hdc and in 2nd ch of turning ch-2—17 (19, 21) hdc. Ch 2, turn.

Row 3:
Sk first hdc, hdc in next 14 (16, 18) hdc, dec over next hdc and 2nd ch of turning ch-2—16 (18, 20) hdc. Ch 2, turn.

Row 4:
Sk first hdc, hdc in each rem hdc and in 2nd ch of turning ch-2. Finish off.

Right Back
Work same as Left Front through Row 20 (22, 22) of armhole shaping.

Row 21 (23, 23):
Sk first hdc, hdc in each rem hdc and in 2nd ch of turning ch-2. Ch 2, turn.

Row 22 (24, 24):
Rep Row 21 (23, 23).

Neckline Shaping:
Row 1 (right side):
Sk first hdc, hdc in next 14 (16, 18) hdc, dec—16 (18, 20) hdc. Ch 2, turn, leaving rem hdc unworked.

Row 2:
Sk first hdc, hdc in each rem hdc and in 2nd ch of turning ch-2. Finish off.

Right Front
With smaller size hook and off white, ch 37 (41, 45).

continued

Row 1 (right side):
Hdc in 3rd ch from hook (2 skipped chs count as an hdc) and in each rem ch—36 (40, 44) hdc. Ch 2 (counts as first hdc on following rows), turn.

Row 2:
Sk first hdc, hdc in each rem hdc and in 2nd ch of beg 2 skipped chs. Ch 2, turn.

Row 3:
Sk first hdc, hdc in each rem hdc and in 2nd ch of turning ch-2. Ch 2, turn.

Rows 4 through 6:
Rep Row 3. At end of Row 6, change to rust. Ch 2, turn.

Row 7:
Sk first hdc, working over off white, hdc in next 9 hdc, change to off white; hdc in each rem hdc and in 2nd ch of turning ch-2. Ch 2, turn.

Row 8:
Sk first hdc, hdc in next 25 (29, 33) hdc; change to rust; hdc in next 9 hdc and in 2nd ch of turning ch-2. Ch 2, turn.

Row 9:
Sk first hdc, hdc in next 9 hdc; change to off white; hdc in each rem hdc and in 2nd ch of turning ch-2. Ch 2, turn.

Rows 10 and 11:
Rep Rows 8 and 9.

Row 12:
Rep Row 8.

Row 13:
Sk first hdc, hdc in next 9 hdc; working over off white, hdc in next 10 hdc, change to off white; hdc in next 15 (19, 23) hdc and in 2nd ch of turning ch-2. Ch 2, turn.

Row 14:
Sk first hdc, hdc in next 15 (19, 23) hdc; change to rust; hdc in each rem hdc and in 2nd ch of turning ch-2. Ch 2, turn.

Row 15:
Sk first hdc, hdc in next 19 hdc; change to off white; hdc in each rem hdc and in 2nd ch of turning ch-2. Ch 2, turn.

Rows 16 and 17:
Rep Rows 14 and 15.

Row 18:
Rep Row 14.

Row 19:
Sk first hdc, hdc in next 19 hdc; working over off white, hdc in next 10 hdc, change to off white; hdc in next 5 (9, 13) hdc and in 2nd ch of turning ch-2. Ch 2, turn.

Row 20:
Sk first hdc, hdc in next 5 (9, 13) hdc; change to rust; hdc in each rem hdc and in 2nd ch of turning ch-2. Ch 2, turn.

Row 21:
Sk first hdc, hdc in next 29 hdc; change to off white; hdc in each rem hdc and in 2nd ch of turning ch-2. Ch 2, turn.

Rows 22 and 23:
Rep Rows 20 and 21.

Row 24:
Rep Row 20.

Row 25:
Sk first hdc, hdc in next 19 hdc; bring off white loosely across unworked rust hdc, change to off white; working over off white, hdc in next 15 (19, 23) hdc and in 2nd ch of turning ch-2. Ch 2, turn.

Row 26:
Sk first hdc, hdc in next 15 (19, 23) hdc; change to rust by drawing lp through; hdc in each rem hdc and in 2nd ch of turning ch-2. Ch 2, turn.

Row 27:
Sk first hdc, hdc in next 19 hdc; change to off white; hdc in each rem hdc and in 2nd ch of turning ch-2. Ch 2, turn.

Rows 28 and 29:
Rep Rows 26 and 27.

Row 30:
Rep Row 26.

Row 31:
Sk first hdc, hdc in next 9 hdc; bring off white loosely across unworked rust hdc; change to off white; working over off white, hdc in next 25 (29, 33) hdc and in 2nd ch of turning ch-2. Ch 2, turn.

Row 32:
Sk first hdc, hdc in next 25 (29, 33) hdc; change to rust; hdc in next 9 hdc and in 2nd ch of turning ch-2. Ch 2, turn.

Row 33:
Sk first hdc, hdc in next 9 hdc; change to off white; hdc in each rem hdc and in 2nd ch of turning ch-2. Ch 2, turn.

Rows 34 and 35:
Rep Rows 32 and 33.

Row 36:
Rep Row 32. At end of row, carry off white loosely across last 10 hdc worked; change to off white. Cut rust. Ch 2, turn.

Row 37:
Sk first hdc, hdc in each rem hdc and in 2nd ch of turning ch-2. Ch 2, turn.

FOR SIZE SMALL ONLY:
Row 38:
Rep Row 37.

Continue with Armhole Shaping on page 41.

Rows 38 through 40:
Rep Row 37.

Continue with Armhole Shaping.

Armhole Shaping:
Row 1 (right side):
Sk first hdc, hdc in next 28 (32, 36) hdc; dec—30 (34, 38) hdc. Ch 2, turn, leaving rem hdc unworked.

Row 2:
Sk first hdc, hdc in each rem hdc and in 2nd ch of turning ch-2. Ch 2, turn.

Row 3:
Sk first hdc, hdc in next 19 (29, 29) hdc; change to rust; hdc in next 9 (3, 7) hdc and in 2nd ch of turning ch-2. Ch 2, turn.

Row 4:
Sk first hdc, hdc in next 9 (3, 7) hdc; change to off white; hdc in each rem hdc and in 2nd ch of turning ch-2. Ch 2, turn.

Rows 5 through 8:
Rep Rows 3 and 4 twice more.

Row 9:
Sk first hdc, hdc in next 9 (19, 19) hdc; bring rust loosely across unworked off white hdc, change to rust; working over rust, hdc in next 19 (13, 17) hdc and in 2nd ch of turning ch-2. Ch 2, turn.

Row 10:
Sk first hdc, hdc in next 19 (13, 17) hdc; change to off white; hdc in each rem hdc and in 2nd ch of turning ch-2. Ch 2, turn.

Row 11:
Sk first hdc, hdc in next 9 (19, 19) hdc; change to rust; hdc in each rem hdc and in 2nd ch of turning ch-2. Ch 2, turn.

Rows 12 and 13:
Rep Rows 10 and 11.

Row14:
Rep Row 10. At end of row, do not ch 2. Change to rust; ch 2, turn.

Row 15:
Sk first hdc, bring rust loosely across unworked off white hdc, change to rust; working over rust, hdc in each hdc and in 2nd ch of turning ch-2. Cut off white. Ch 2, turn.

Row 16:
Sk first hdc, hdc in each hdc and in 2nd ch of turning ch-2. Ch 2, turn.

Rows 17 through 20:
Rep Row 16. At end of Row 20, ch 1, turn.

Continue with Neckline Shaping below.

Row 15:
Sk first hdc, hdc in next 9 hdc; bring rust loosely across unworked off white hdc, change to rust by drawing lp through; working over rust, hdc in next 23 (27) hdc and in 2nd ch of turning ch-2. Ch 2, turn.

Row 16:
Sk first hdc, hdc in next 23 (27) hdc; change to off white; hdc in next 9 hdc and in 2nd ch of turning ch-2. Ch 2, turn.

Row 17:
Sk first hdc, hdc in next 9 hdc; change to rust; hdc in each rem hdc and in 2nd ch of turning ch-2. Ch 2, turn.

Rows 18 and 19:
Rep Rows 16 and 17.

Row 20:
Rep Row 16. At end of row, bring rust loosely across unworked off white hdc; change to rust. Cut off white. Ch 2, turn.

Row 21:
Sk first hdc, hdc in each rem hdc and in 2nd ch of turning ch-2. Ch 2, turn.

Row 22:
Sk first hdc, hdc in each rem hdc and in 2nd ch of turning ch-2. Ch 1, turn.

Continue with Neckline Shaping.

Neckline Shaping:
Row 1:
Sl st in first 13 (15, 17) hdc, ch 2 (counts as an hdc), hdc in each rem hdc and in 2nd ch of turning ch-2—18 (20, 22) hdc. Ch 2, turn.

Row 2:
Sk next hdc, hdc in next 15 hdc, dec over next hdc and 2nd ch of beg ch-2—17 (19, 21) hdc. Ch 2, turn.

Row 3:
Sk first hdc, dec; hdc in each rem hdc and in 2nd ch of turning ch-2—16 (18, 20) hdc. Ch 2, turn.

Row 4:
Sk first hdc, hdc in each hdc and in 2nd ch of turning ch-2. Finish off.

Left Back
Work same as Right Front through Row 20 (22, 22) of armhole shaping. At end of Row 20 (22, 22), ch 2, turn.

Row 21 (23, 23):
Sk first hdc, hdc in each hdc and in 2nd ch of turning ch-2. Ch 2, turn.

continued

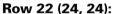

Row 22 (24, 24):
Sk first hdc, hdc in each hdc and in 2nd ch of turning ch-2. Ch 1, turn.

Neckline Shaping:
Row 1 (right side**):**
Sl st in first 14 hdc, ch 2, dec; hdc in each rem hdc and in 2nd ch of turning ch-2—16 **(**18, 20**)** hdc. Ch 2, turn.

Row 2:
Sk first hdc, hdc in each rem hdc and in 2nd ch of beg ch-2. Finish off.

Left Sleeve
With smaller size hook and rust, ch 42 **(**46, 46**)**.

Row 1:
Hdc in 3rd ch from hook **(**beg 2 skipped chs count as an hdc**)** and in each rem ch—41 **(**45, 45**)** hdc. Ch 2 **(**counts as first hdc on following rows**)**, turn.

Row 2:
Sk first hdc, hdc in each rem hdc and in 2nd ch of beg 2 skipped chs. Ch 2, turn.

Row 3:
Sk first hdc, hdc in each rem hdc and in 2nd ch of turning ch-2. Ch 2, turn.

Row 4:
Hdc in first hdc and in each rem hdc to turning ch-2; 2 hdc in 2nd ch of turning ch-2—43 **(**47, 47**)** hdc. Ch 2, turn.

Rows 5 through 7:
Rep Row 3.

Row 8:
Rep Row 4.

Rows 9 through 32:
Rep Rows 5 through 8 six times more.

Rows 33 through 35:
Rep Row 5.

FOR SIZE SMALL ONLY:
Row 36:
Hdc in first hdc and in each rem hdc to turning ch-2; 2 hdc in 2nd ch of turning ch-2—59 hdc. Ch 1, turn.

Continue with Armhole Shaping.

FOR SIZES MEDIUM AND LARGE ONLY:
Row 36:
Hdc in first dc and in each rem hdc to turning ch-2; 2 hdc in 2nd ch of turning ch-2—63 **(**63**)** sts. Ch 3, turn.

Row 37:
Sk first hdc, hdc in each rem hdc and in 2nd ch of turning ch-2. Ch 2, turn.

Row 38:
Sk first hdc, hdc in each rem hdc and in 2nd ch of turning ch-2. Ch 1, turn.

Continue with Armhole Shaping.

Armhole Shaping:
Row 1 (right side**):**
Sl st in first 6 hdc, ch 2 (counts as an hdc), hdc in next 48 **(**52, 52**)** hdc—49 **(**53, 53**)** hdc. Ch 2, turn, leaving rem sts unworked.

Row 2:
Sk first hdc, hdc in each hdc to last hdc and beg ch-2; dec over last hdc and 2nd ch of beg ch-2—47 **(**51, 51**)** sts. Ch 2, turn.

Row 3:
Sk first hdc, hdc in each hdc to last 2 hdc and turning ch-2; dec over last 2 hdc—45 **(**49, 49**)** hdc. Ch 2, turn, leaving turning ch-2 unworked.

Rows 4 through 24 (26, 26):
Rep Row 3. At end of Row 24 **(**26, 26**)**—3 hdc. At end of last row, do not ch 2. Finish off.

Right Sleeve
With smaller size hook and off white, ch 42 **(**46, 46**)**.

Work same as Left Sleeve.

Weave in all ends.

Finishing
Step 1:
Hold right and left front pieces with wrong sides together and beginning chain to right. With rust and beginning with Row 9, sew center seam with overcast stitch (see Stitch Guide on page 5), carefully matching rows. Sew center back seam in same manner, beginning at lower edge.

Step 2:
Sew shoulder seams.

Step 3:
Sew white sleeve in left armhole opening having last row of sleeve at shoulder seam, matching pattern and easing as necessary to fit. Repeat with rust sleeve in right armhole opening.

Step 4:
Sew sleeve and side seams matching pattern.

Step 5:

For Center Front and Back Trim, hold sweater with right side of front facing you. Holding one strand of each color together and keeping yarn behind work, join in joining of center front seam at Row 9. Insert larger size hook from front to back through same sp, draw up a lp and draw through lp on hook to form a ch. Working *loosely*, continue to work chs over center front seam. Finish off and weave in ends. Repeat over center back seam, beginning at lower edge and ending at neckline. Finish off.

Step 6:

For Neckline Trim, hold sweater with right side facing you and left shoulder seam at top. Holding one strand of each color together, make lp on hook and join with an sc in left shoulder seam. Working in reverse sc (see Stitch Guide on page 5) around neckline and drawing up lps ½", sk next st; * sc in next st, sk next st; rep from * around neckline, working in every other st and in each edge hdc; join in joining sc. Finish off and weave in all ends.

Step 7:

For Lower Edge Trim, hold sweater with right side facing you and beginning chain of left back at top. Holding one strand of each color together, make lp on hook and join with an sc in first unused lp of left back. Working in reverse sc in remaining unused lps along lower edge and drawing up lps ½", sk next lp; * reverse sc in next lp, sk next lp; rep from * to center front; reverse sc in each edge hdc of Rows 1 through 8 of left front and each edge hdc of Rows 8 through 1 of right front; continuing along lower edge, ** reverse sc in next unused lp, sk next unused lp; rep from ** to joining; join in joining sc. Finish off and weave in ends.

Step 8:

For Sleeve Trim, hold one sleeve with right side facing you and beginning chain at top. Holding one strand of each color together, make lp on hook and join with an sc in seam. Working in reverse sc in unused lps of beginning chain and drawing up lps ½", sk next lp; * reverse sc in next lp, sk next lp; rep from * around; join in joining sc. Finish off. Repeat for other sleeve. Weave in all ends.

Sophisticated Stripe Sweater

designed by Hélène Rush

Sizes:

	Small	Medium	Large
Chest Measurement:	30"-32"	34"-36"	38"-40"
Finished Chest Measurement:	38"	42"	46"

Note: Instructions are written for size small; changes for larger sizes are in parentheses.

Materials:

Patons Cotton d.k. (1.75 oz ball), 7 (8, 9) balls each Black #3696 and Ecru #3681; 5 (6, 7) balls Sand #3651—or other sport weight yarn worked to gauge

Size H (5mm) crochet hook, or size required for gauge

Three ¾" diameter buttons

Sewing needle and matching thread

Size 16 tapestry needle

Gauge:

Note: See "A Word about Gauge" on page 5.

9 sc = 2"

5 sc rows = 1"

In pattern:

18 sts = 4"

17 rows = 4"

continued

All measurements are approximate.

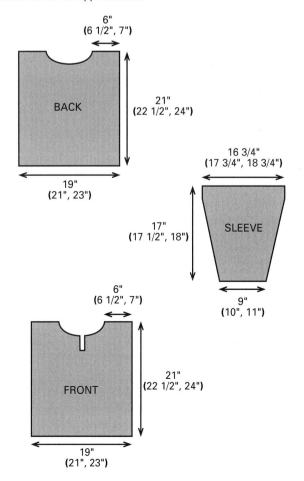

Color photograph, front cover

Pattern Stitch

Long Double Crochet (long dc):
YO, insert hook in sc indicated on 3rd row below, draw up lp to height of working row, (YO and draw through 2 lps on hook) twice—long dc made.
Note: Always skip st behind long dc on working row.

Instructions

Back

Note: When changing color at end of row work until 2 lps of last st rem on hook, with new color, YO and draw through 2 lps on hook. Cut old color.

With black, ch 88 (96, 104).

Row 1 (right side):
Dc in 4th ch from hook (beg 3 skipped chs count as a dc) and in each ch—86 (94, 102) dc. Ch 1, turn.

Row 2:
Sc in first dc, in each rem dc and in 3rd ch of beg 3 skipped chs, changing to ecru in last sc. Ch 3 (counts as first dc on following rows), turn.

Row 3:
Sk first dc, dc in next sc; * ch 2, sk next 2 sc, dc in next 2 sc; rep from * 20 (22, 24) times more. Ch 1, turn.

Row 4:
Sc in first 2 dc, 2 sc in next ch-2 sp; * sc in next 2 dc, 2 sc in next ch-2 sp; rep from * 19 (21, 23) times more; sc in next dc and in 3rd ch of turning ch-3, changing to sand in last sc. Ch 2 (counts as first hdc on following rows), turn.

Row 5:
Sk first sc, hdc in next sc, long dc (see Pattern Stitch) in each of next 2 skipped sc on 3rd row below; * hdc in next 2 sc, long dc in each of next 2 skipped sc on 3rd row below; rep from * 19 (21, 23) times more; hdc in next 2 sc. Ch 1, turn.

Row 6:
Sc in first hdc, in each rem hdc, in each long dc, and in 2nd ch of turning ch-2, changing to black in last sc. Ch 3, turn.

Row 7:
Sk first sc, dc in each rem sc. Ch 1, turn.

Row 8:
Sc in first dc, in each rem dc, and in 3rd ch of turning ch-3, changing to ecru in last sc. Ch 3, turn.

Rows 9 through 80 (86, 92):
Rep Rows 3 through 8, 12 (13, 14) times.

Right Neck Shaping:

FOR SIZES SMALL AND LARGE ONLY:

Row 1 (right side):
Sk first sc, dc in next sc; * ch 2, sk next 2 sc, dc in next 2 sc; rep from * 5 (6) times more; dc in next sc, dec over next 2 sc [to work dec: (YO, draw up lp in next st, YO and draw through 2 lps on hook) twice; YO and draw through all 3 lps on hook—dec made]; dc in next sc—6 (7) ch-2 sps. Ch 1, turn, leaving rem sts unworked.

Row 2:
Sc in first dc, sc dec over next 2 sts (to work sc dec: draw up lp in each of next 2 sts, YO and draw through all 3 lps on hook—sc dec made); * sc in next 2 dc, 2 sc in next ch-2 sp; rep from * 5 (6) times more; sc in next dc and in 3rd ch of turning ch-3, changing to sand in last sc—28 (32) sc. Ch 2, turn.

Row 3:
Sk first sc, hdc in next sc; * long dc in each of next 2 skipped sc on 3rd row below, hdc in next 2 sc; rep from * 5 (6) times more; hdc in next 2 sc. Ch 1, turn.

Row 4:
Sc in first hdc, in each rem hdc, in each long dc, and in 2nd ch of turning ch-2, changing to black in last sc. Ch 3, turn.

Row 5:
Sk first sc, dc in each rem sc. Ch 1, turn.

Row 6:
Sc in first dc, in each rem dc, and in 3rd ch of turning ch-3, changing to ecru in last sc. Ch 3, turn.

Row 7:
Sk first sc, dc in next sc; * ch 2, sk next 2 sc, dc in next 2 sc; rep from * 5 (6) times more; dc in next 2 sc. Ch 1, turn.

Row 8:
Sc in first 4 dc; * 2 sc in next ch-2 sp; sc in next 2 dc; rep from * 4 (5) times more; 2 sc in next ch-2 sp; sc in next dc and in 3rd ch of turning ch-3, changing to sand in last sc.

Row 9:
Rep Row 3.

Row 10:
Sc in first hdc, in each rem hdc, in each long dc, and in 2nd ch of turning ch-2. Finish off.

Continue with Left Neck Shaping.

FOR SIZE MEDIUM ONLY:
Row 1 (right side):
Sk first sc, dc in next sc; * ch 2, sk next 2 sc, dc in next 2 sc; rep from * 5 times more; ch 2, sk next 2 sc, dc in next sc, dec over next 2 sc [to work dec: (YO, draw up lp in next st, YO and draw through 2 lps on hook) twice; YO and draw through all 3 lps on hook—dec made]; dc in next sc—7 ch-2 sps. Ch 1, turn, leaving rem sts unworked.

Row 2:
Sc in first dc, sc dec over next 2 sts (to work sc dec: draw up lp in each of next 2 sts, YO and draw through all 3 lps on hook—sc dec made); * 2 sc in next ch-2 sp; sc in next 2 dc; rep from * 5 times more; 2 sc in next ch-2 sp; sc in next dc and in 3rd ch of turning ch-3, changing to sand in last sc—30 sc. Ch 2, turn.

Row 3:
Sk first sc, hdc in next sc, long dc in each of next 2 skipped sc on 3rd row below; * hdc in next 2 sc, long dc in each of next 2 skipped sc on 3rd row below; rep from * 5 times more; hdc in next 2 sc. Ch 1, turn.

Row 4:
Sc in first hdc, in each rem hdc, in each long dc, and in 2nd ch of turning ch-2, changing to black in last sc. Ch 3, turn.

Row 5:
Sk first sc, dc in each rem sc. Ch 1, turn.

Row 6:
Sc in first dc, in each rem dc, and in 3rd ch of turning ch-3, changing to ecru in last sc. Ch 3, turn.

Row 7:
Sk first sc, dc in next sc; * ch 2, sk next 2 sc, dc in next 2 sc; rep from * 6 times more. Ch 1, turn.

Row 8:
Sc in first 2 dc, 2 sc in next ch-2 sp; * sc in next 2 dc, 2 sc in next ch-2 sp; rep from * 5 times more; sc in next dc and in 3rd ch of turning ch-3, changing to sand in last sc. Ch 2, turn.

Row 9:
Rep Row 3.

Row 10:
Sc in first hdc, in each rem hdc, in each long dc and in 2nd ch of turning ch-2. Finish off.

Continue with Left Neck Shaping.

Left Neck Shaping:

FOR SIZES SMALL AND LARGE ONLY:
Hold back with right side facing you; sk next 26 (34) sts from right neck shaping, join ecru in next sc.

Row 1 (right side):
Ch 3 (counts as a dc), dec over next 2 sc; dc in next 3 sc; * ch 2, sk next 2 sc, dc in next 2 sc; rep from * 5 (6) times more—6 (7) ch-2 sps. Ch 1, turn.

Row 2:
Sc in first 2 dc; * 2 sc in next ch-2 sp; sc in next 2 dc; rep from * 5 (6) times more; sc dec over next 2 sts; sc in 3rd ch of beg ch-3, changing to sand—28 (32) sc. Ch 2, turn.

Row 3:
Sk first sc, dc in next 3 sc; * long dc in each of next 2 skipped sc on 3rd row below; hdc in next 2 sc; rep from * 5 (6) times more. Ch 1, turn.

Row 4:
Sc in first hdc, in each rem hdc, in each long dc, and in 2nd ch of turning ch-2, changing to black in last sc. Ch 3, turn.

Row 5:
Sk first sc, dc in each rem sc. Ch 1, turn.

Row 6:
Sc in first dc, in each rem dc, and in 3rd ch of turning ch-3, changing to ecru in last sc. Ch 3, turn.

Row 7:
Sk first sc, dc in next 3 sc; * ch 2, sk next 2 sc, dc in next 2 sc; rep from * 5 (6) times more. Ch 1, turn.

Row 8:
Sc in first 2 dc; * 2 sc in next ch-2 sp; sc in next 2 dc; rep from * 5 (6) times more; sc in next dc and in 3rd ch of turning ch-3, changing to sand in last sc. Ch 2, turn.

Row 9:
Rep Row 3.

Row 10:
Sc in first hdc, in each rem hdc, in each long dc, and in 2nd ch of turning ch-2.

Finish off and weave in all ends.

Continue with Front on page 46.

FOR SIZE MEDIUM ONLY:
Hold back with right side facing you, sk next 30 sts from right neck shaping, join ecru in next sc.

continued

Row 1 (right side):
Ch 3 (counts as a dc), dec over next 2 sc; dc in next sc;
* ch 2, sk next 2 sc, dc in next 2 sc; rep from * 6 times
more—7 ch-2 sps. Ch 1, turn.

Row 2:
Sc in first 2 dc; * 2 sc in next ch-2 sp; sc in next 2 dc; rep
from * 5 times more; 2 sc in next ch-2 sp; sc dec over next
2 sts; sc in next dc, changing to sand—30 sc. Ch 2, turn.

Row 3:
Sk first sc, hdc in next sc, long dc in each of next
2 skipped sc on 3rd row below; * hdc in next 2 sc, long dc
in each of next 2 skipped sc on 3rd row below; rep from
* 5 times more; hdc in next 2 sc. Ch 1, turn.

Row 4:
Sc in first hdc, in each rem hdc, in each long dc, and in
2nd ch of turning ch-2, changing to black in last sc.
Ch 3, turn.

Row 5:
Sk first sc, dc in each rem sc. Ch 1, turn.

Row 6:
Sc in first dc, in each rem dc, and in 3rd ch of turning ch-3,
changing to ecru in last sc. Ch 3, turn.

Row 7:
Sk first sc, dc in next sc; * ch 2, sk next 2 sc, dc in next
2 sc; rep from * 6 times more. Ch 1, turn.

Row 8:
Sc in first 2 dc; * 2 sc in next ch-2 sp; sc in next 2 dc; rep
from * 5 times more; 2 sc in next ch-2 sp; sc in next dc
and in 3rd ch of turning ch-3, changing to sand in last sc.
Ch 2, turn.

Row 9:
Rep Row 3.

Row 10:
Sc in first hdc, in each rem hdc, in each long dc, and in
2nd ch of turning ch-2.

Finish off and weave in all ends.

Front
With black, ch 88 (96, 104).

Rows 1 through 8:
Rep Rows 1 through 8 of Back.

Rows 9 through 56 (62, 68):
Rep Rows 3 through 8 of Back, 8 (9, 10) times.

Left Placket Shaping:
Row 1 (right side):
Sk first sc, dc in next sc; * ch 2, sk next 2 sc, dc in next
2 sc; rep from * 8 (9, 10) times more; ch 2, sk next 2 sc, dc
in next sc. Ch 1, turn, leaving rem sts unworked.

Row 2:
Sc in first dc; * 2 sc in next ch-2 sp; sc in next 2 dc; rep
from * 8 (9, 10) times more; 2 sc in next ch-2 sp; sc in next
dc and in 3rd ch of turning ch-3, changing to sand in last
sc. Ch 2, turn.

Row 3:
Sk first sc, hdc in next sc, long dc in each of next
2 skipped sc on 3rd row below; * hdc in next 2 sc, long dc
in each of next 2 skipped sc on 3rd row below; rep from
* 8 (9, 10) times more; hdc in next sc. Ch 1, turn.

Row 4:
Sc in first hdc, in each long dc, in each hdc, and in 2nd ch
of turning ch-2, changing to black in last sc. Ch 3, turn.

Row 5:
Sk first sc, dc in each rem sc. Ch 1, turn.

Row 6:
Sc in first dc, in each rem dc, and in 3rd ch of turning ch-
3, changing to ecru in last sc. Ch 3, turn.

Row 7:
Sk first sc, dc in next sc; * ch 2, sk next 2 sc, dc in next
2 sc; rep from * 8 (9, 10) times more; ch 2, sk next 2 sc, dc
in next sc. Ch 1, turn.

Rows 8 through 19:
Rep Rows 2 through 7 twice more.

Rows 20 through 23:
Rep Rows 2 through 5.

Neck Shaping:
Row 1 (wrong side):
Sl st in first 9 (11, 13) dc, ch 1, sc in same dc as last sl st
made, in each rem dc, and in 3rd ch of turning ch-3,
changing to ecru in last sc—33 (35, 37) sc. Ch 3, turn.

FOR SIZES SMALL AND LARGE ONLY:
Row 2 (right side):
Sk first sc, dc in next sc; * ch 2, sk next 2 sc, dc in next
2 sc; rep from * 6 (7) times more; dec over next 2 sc; dc in
next sc. Ch 1, turn.

Row 3:
Sc in first dc, sc dec over next 2 sts; sc in next dc; * 2 sc in
next ch-2 sp; sc in next 2 dc; rep from * 5 (6) times more;
2 sc in next ch-2 sp; sc in next dc and in 3rd ch of turning
ch-3, changing to sand in last sc. Ch 2, turn.

Row 4:
Sk first sc, hdc in next sc, long dc in each of next
2 skipped sc on 3rd row below; * hdc in next 2 sc, long dc
in each of next 2 skipped sc on 3rd row below; rep from
* 5 (6) times more; hdc dec over next 2 sc [to work hdc
dec: (YO, draw up lp in next sc) twice; YO and draw
through all 5 lps on hook—hdc dec made]; hdc in next sc.
Ch 1, turn.

Row 5:
Sc in first hdc, sc dec over next 2 sts; sc in each hdc, in each long dc, and in 2nd ch of turning ch-2, changing to black in last sc—28 (32) sc. Ch 3, turn.

Row 6:
Sk first sc, dc in each rem sc. Ch 1, turn.

Row 7:
Sc in first dc, in each rem dc, and in 3rd ch of turning ch-3, changing to ecru in last sc. Ch 3, turn.

Row 8:
Sk first sc, dc in next sc; * ch 2, sk next 2 sc, dc in next 2 sc; rep from * 5 (6) times more; ch 1, sk next sc, dc in next sc. Ch 1, turn.

Row 9:
Sc in first dc and in next ch-1 sp; * sc in next 2 dc, 2 sc in next ch-2 sp; rep from * 5 (6) times more; sc in next dc and in 3rd ch of turning ch-3, changing to sand in last sc. Ch 2, turn.

Row 10:
Sk first hdc, hdc in next sc; * long dc in each of next 2 skipped sc on 3rd row below; hdc in next 2 sc; rep from * 5 (6) times more; long dc in next skipped sc on 3rd row below; hdc in next sc. Ch 1, turn.

Row 11:
Sc in first hdc, in each rem hdc, in each long dc, and in 2nd ch of turning ch-2. Finish off.

Continue with Right Placket Shaping.

FOR SIZE MEDIUM ONLY:
Row 2 (right side):
Sk first sc, dc in next sc; * ch 2, sk next 2 sc; dc in next 2 sc; rep from * 6 times more; ch 1, sk next sc, dc in next sc, dec over next 2 sc; dc in next sc. Ch 1, turn.

Row 3:
Sc in first dc, sc dec over next 2 sts; sc in next dc, sc in next ch-1 sp; * sc in next 2 dc, 2 sc in next ch-2 sp; rep from * 6 times more; sc in next dc and in 3rd ch of turning ch-3, changing to sand in last sc. Ch 2, turn.

Row 4:
Sk first sc, hdc in next sc, long dc in each of next 2 skipped sc on 3rd row below; * hdc in next 2 sc, long dc in each of next 2 skipped sc on 3rd row below; rep from * 5 times more; hdc in next 2 sc, hdc dec over next 2 sc [to work hdc dec: (YO, draw up lp in next sc) twice; YO and draw through all 5 lps on hook—hdc dec made]; hdc in next sc. Ch 1, turn.

Row 5:
Sc in first hdc, sc dec over next 2 sts; sc in each hdc, in each long dc, and in 2nd ch of turning ch-2, changing to black in last sc—30 sts. Ch 3, turn.

Row 6:
Sk first sc, dc in each rem sc. Ch 1, turn.

Row 7:
Sc in first dc, in each rem dc, and in 3rd ch of turning ch-3, changing to ecru in last sc. Ch 3, turn.

Row 8:
Sk first sc, dc in next sc; * ch 2, sk next 2 sc, dc in next 2 sc; rep from * 6 times more. Ch 1, turn.

Row 9:
Sc in first 2 dc, 2 sc in next ch-2 sp; * sc in next 2 dc, 2 sc in next ch-2 sp; rep from * 5 times more; sc in next dc and in 3rd ch of turning ch-3, changing to sand in last sc. Ch 2, turn.

Row 10:
Sk first sc, hdc in next sc; * long dc in each of next 2 skipped sc on 3rd row below; hdc in next 2 sc; rep from * 6 times more. Ch 1, turn.

Row 11:
Sc in first hdc, in each rem hdc, in each long dc, and in 2nd ch of turning ch-2. Finish off.

Continue with Right Placket Shaping.

Right Placket Shaping:

Hold Front with right side facing you; sk next 4 sc from left placket shaping, join ecru in next sc.

Row 1 (right side):
Ch 5 (counts as a dc and a ch-2 sp), sk next 3 sc; * dc in next 2 sc, ch 2, sk next 2 sc; rep from * 8 (9,10) times more; dc in next 2 sc. Ch 1, turn.

Row 2:
Sc in first 2 dc; * 2 sc in next ch-2 sp; sc in next 2 dc; rep from * 8 (9,10) times more; sc in next 3 chs of beg ch-5, changing to sand in last sc. Ch 2 (counts as first hdc on following rows), turn.

Row 3:
Sk first sc, long dc in each of next 2 skipped sc on 3rd row below; * hdc in next 2 sc, long dc in each of next 2 skipped sc on 3rd row below; rep from * 8 (9, 10) times more; hdc in next 2 sc. Ch 1, turn.

Row 4:
Sc in first hdc, in each rem hdc, in each long dc, and in 2nd ch of turning ch-2, changing to black in last sc. Ch 3, turn.

Row 5:
Sk first sc, dc in each rem sc. Ch 1, turn.

continued

Row 6:
Sc in first dc, in each rem dc, and in 3rd ch of turning ch-3, changing to ecru in last sc. Ch 5, turn.

Row 7:
Sk first 3 sc; * dc in next 2 sc, ch 2, sk next 2 sc; rep from * 8 (9, 10) times more; dc in next 2 sc. Ch 1, turn.

Rows 8 through 19:
Rep Rows 2 through 7 twice more.

Rows 20 through 23:
Rep Rows 2 through 5.

Neck Shaping:
Row 1 (wrong side):
Sc in first dc and in next 32 (34, 36) dc, changing to ecru in last sc—33 (35, 37) sc. Ch 3, turn, leaving rem sts unworked.

FOR SIZES SMALL AND LARGE ONLY:
Row 2 (right side):
Sk first sc, dec over next 2 sc; * dc in next 2 sc, ch 2, sk next 2 sc; rep from * 6 (7) times more; dc in next 2 sc. Ch 1, turn.

Row 3:
Sc in first 2 dc; * 2 sc in next ch-2 sp; sc in next 2 dc; rep from * 5 (6) times more; 2 sc in next ch-2 sp; sc in next dc, sc dec over next 2 sts; sc in 3rd ch of turning ch-3, changing to sand in last sc. Ch 2, turn.

Row 4:
Sk first sc, hdc dec over next 2 sts; * long dc in each of next 2 skipped sc on 3rd row below; hdc in next 2 sc; rep from * 6 (7) times more. Ch 1, turn.

Row 5:
Sc in first hdc, in each rem hdc, and in each long dc to last 2 hdc and turning ch-2; sc dec over last 2 hdc; sc in 2nd ch of turning ch-2, changing to black in last sc—28 (32) sc. Ch 3, turn.

Row 6:
Sk first sc, dc in each rem sc. Ch 1, turn.

Row 7:
Sc in first dc, in each rem dc, and in 3rd ch of turning ch-3, changing to ecru in last sc. Ch 4 (counts as first dc and ch-1 sp on following row), turn.

Row 8:
Sk first 2 sc; * dc in next 2 sc, ch 2, sk next 2 sc; rep from * 5 (6) times more; dc in next 2 sc. Ch 1, turn.

Row 9:
Sc in first 2 dc; * 2 sc in next ch-2 sp; sc in next 2 dc; rep from * 5 (6) times more; sc in next 2 chs of turning ch-4, changing to sand in last sc. Ch 2, turn.

Row 10:
Sk first sc, long dc in next skipped sc on 3rd row below; * hdc in next 2 dc, long dc in each of next 2 skipped sc on 3rd row below; rep from * 5 (6) times more; hdc in next 2 sc. Ch 1, turn.

Row 11:
Sc in first hdc, in each rem hdc, in each long dc, and in 2nd ch of turning ch-2.

Finish off and weave in all ends.

Continue with Sleeve on page 49.

FOR SIZE MEDIUM ONLY:
Row 2 (right side):
Sk first sc, dec over next 2 sc; dc in next sc, ch 1, sk next sc; * dc in next 2 sc, ch 2, sk next 2 sc; rep from * 6 times more; dc in next 2 sc. Ch 1, turn.

Row 3:
Sc in first 2 dc; * 2 sc in next ch-2 sp; sc in next 2 dc; rep from * 6 times more; sc in next ch-1 sp, sc dec over next 2 sts; sc in 3rd ch of turning ch-3, changing to sand in last sc. Ch 2, turn.

Row 4:
Sk first sc, hdc dec over next 2 sts; * hdc in next 2 sc, long dc in each of next 2 skipped sc on 3rd row below; rep from * 6 times more; hdc in next 2 sc. Ch 1, turn.

Row 5:
Sc in first hdc, in each rem hdc, and in each long dc to last 2 hdc and turning ch-2; sc dec over last 2 hdc; sc in 2nd ch of turning ch-2, changing to black in last sc—30 sts. Ch 3, turn.

Row 6:
Sk first sc, dc in each rem sc. Ch 1, turn.

Row 7:
Sc in first dc, in each rem dc, and in 3rd ch of turning ch-3, changing to ecru in last sc. Ch 3, turn.

Row 8:
Sk first sc, dc in next sc; * ch 2, sk next 2 sc, dc in next 2 sc; rep from * 6 times more. Ch 1, turn.

Row 9:
Sc in first 2 dc, 2 sc in next ch-2 sp; * sc in next 2 dc, 2 sc in next ch-2 sp; rep from * 5 times more; sc in next dc and in 3rd ch of turning ch-3, changing to sand in last sc. Ch 2, turn.

Row 10:
Sk first sc, hdc in next sc; * long dc in each of next 2 skipped sc on 3rd row below; hdc in next 2 sc; rep from * 6 times more. Ch 1, turn.

Row 11:
Sc in first hdc, in each rem hdc, in each long dc, and in 2nd ch of turning ch-2.

Finish off and weave in all ends.

Sleeve (make 2)
With black, ch 44 (48, 52).

Row 1 (right side):
Dc in 4th ch from hook (beg 3 skipped chs count as a dc) and in each rem ch—42 (46, 50) dc. Ch 1, turn.

Row 2:
Sc in first dc, in each rem dc, and in 3rd ch of beg 3 skipped chs, changing to ecru in last sc. Ch 3 (counts as first dc on following rows), turn.

Row 3:
Sk first sc, dc in next sc; * ch 2, sk next 2 sc, dc in next 2 sc; rep from * 9 (10, 11) times more. Ch 1, turn.

Row 4:
Sc in first 2 dc, 2 sc in next ch-2 sp; * sc in next 2 dc, 2 sc in next ch-2 sp; rep from * 8 (9, 10) times more; sc in next dc and in 3rd ch of turning ch-3, changing to sand in last dc. Ch 2 (counts as first hdc on following rows), turn.

Row 5:
Hdc in first 2 sc, long dc in each of next 2 skipped sc on 3rd row below; * hdc in next 2 sc, long dc in each of next 2 skipped sc on 3rd row below; rep from * 8 (9, 10) times more; hdc in next sc, 2 hdc in next sc—44 (48, 52) sts. Ch 1, turn.

Row 6:
Sc in first hdc, in each rem hdc, in each long dc, and in 2nd ch of turning ch-2, changing to black in last sc. Ch 3, turn.

Row 7:
Sk first sc, dc in each rem sc. Ch 1, turn.

Row 8:
Sc in first dc, in each rem dc, and in 3rd ch of turning ch-3, changing to ecru in last sc. Ch 3, turn.

Row 9:
Dc in first sc and in next 2 sc; * ch 2, sk next 2 sc; dc in next 2 sc; rep from * 9 (10, 11) times more; 2 dc in next sc. Ch 1, turn.

Row 10:
Sc in first 4 dc; * 2 sc in next ch-2 sp; sc in next 2 dc; rep from * 9 (10, 11) times more; sc in next dc and in 3rd ch of turning ch-3, changing to sand in last sc. Ch 2, turn.

Row 11:
Sk first sc, hdc in next 3 sc; * long dc in next 2 skipped sc on 3rd row below; hdc in next 2 sc; rep from * 9 (10, 11) times more; hdc in next 2 sc. Ch 1, turn.

Row 12:
Sc in first hdc, in each rem hdc, in each long dc, and in 2nd ch of turning ch-2, changing to black in last sc. Ch 3, turn.

Row 13:
Dc in first sc and in each sc to last sc; 2 dc in last sc—48 (52, 56) dc. Ch 1, turn.

Row 14:
Sc in first dc, in each rem dc, and in 3rd ch of turning ch-3, changing to ecru in last sc. Ch 3, turn.

Note: Work inc at each end as an sc, hdc or dc until sts can be incorporated into pattern.

Continue in pattern as established inc one st each end of every 4th row 8 (9, 10) times more—64 (70, 76) sts; then inc one st each end of every other row 6 (5, 4) times—76 (80, 84) sts.

Work even until sleeve measures 17" (17 1/2", 18") from beg, ending by working a wrong side row.

Finish off and weave in all ends.

Sew shoulder seams.

Neck Band:
Hold sweater with right side of right front facing you; with black, make lp on hook and join with an sc in first unused dc on right front neck edge.

Row 1:
Sc in next 7 (9, 11) dc; working along neck edge, sc in edge st of next row; † 2 sc in edge of next row; sc in edge of next row †; rep from † to † 4 times more; sc in right shoulder seam; working along right back neck edge, sc in edge of next row; rep from † to † 5 times; working across back neck edge, sc in next 26 (30, 34) sts; working along left back next edge, sc in edge of next row; rep from † to † 5 times; sc in left shoulder seam; working along left front neck edge, sc in edge of next row; rep from † to † 5 times; working along left neck edge, sc in next 8 (10, 12) sts—108 (116, 124) sc. Ch 1, turn.

Row 2:
Sc in each sc. Ch 1, turn.

Row 3:
Sc in each sc. Finish off.

Left Placket Edging:
Hold sweater with right side of left front facing you and neck edge to right. With black, make lp on hook and join with an sc in edge sc of Row 3 of neck band.

Row 1:
Working along neck band and placket edge in sps formed by edge sts, sc in edge of each row—26 sc. Ch 1, turn.

Row 2:
Sc in each sc. Ch 1, turn.

Rows 3 through 6:
Rep Row 2. At end of Row 6, do not ch 1. Finish off.

continued

49

Right Placket Edging:
Hold sweater with right side of right front facing you and neck edge to left; with black, make lp on hook and join with an sc in edge of first row of placket.

Row 1:
Working along placket and neck band edge in sps formed by edge sts, sc in edge of each row—26 sc. Ch 1, turn.

Row 2:
Sc in each sc. Ch 1, turn.

Row 3:
Rep Row 2.

Row 4:
Sc in first 4 sc, ch 2, sk next 2 sc—buttonhole made; * sc in next 7 sc, ch 2, sk next 2 sc—buttonhole made; rep from * once more; sc in next 2 sc. Ch 1, turn.

Row 5:
Sc in first 2 sc, 2 sc next ch-2 sp; * sc in next 7 sc, 2 sc in next ch-2 sp; rep from * once more; sc in next 4 sc. Ch 1, turn.

Row 6:
Sc in each sc. Finish off.

Neck Border:
Hold sweater with right side of left front neck band facing you; with black, make lp on hook and join with an sc in edge of Row 6 of left placket edging; work reverse sc (see Stitch Guide on page 5) in edge of each row of left placket edging, in each sc around neck edge, and in edge of each row of right placket edging.

Finish off and weave in ends.

Finishing
Step 1:
Measure 8$\frac{1}{2}$" (9", 9$\frac{1}{2}$") on each side of shoulder seam and place markers on armhole edge. Sew Sleeves between markers, easing to fit.

Step 2:
Sew sleeve and side seams matching pattern.

Step 3:
Place Right Placket edging over Left Placket edging and stitch lower edge to front edge through all 3 layers.

Step 4:
Sew buttons opposite buttonholes.

Summertime Tee

designed by Melissa Leapman

Sizes:

	Small	Medium	Large
Chest Measurement:	30"-32"	34"-36"	38"-40"
Finished Chest Measurement:	35"	40"	45"

Note: Instructions are written for size small; changes for larger sizes are in parentheses.

Materials:

Coats and Clark Southmaid Cotton 8 (2.5 oz skein), 4 (5, 6) skeins Royal #819; 4 (4, 5) skeins White #3801—or other sport weight yarn worked to gauge
Size F (3.75mm) crochet hook, or size required for gauge
Size G (4.25mm) crochet hook
Size 16 tapestry needle

Gauge:

Note: See "A Word about Gauge" on page 5.
With smaller size hook:
5 sc = 1"
5 sc rows = 1"
In pattern with smaller size hook:
19 sts = 4"
15 rows = 4"

All measurements are approximate.

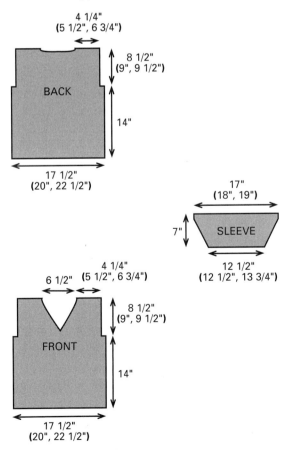

Instructions

Note: When changing colors at end of row, work until 2 lps of last st rem on hook; with new color, YO and draw through 2 lps on hook. Carry color not in use loosely along edge of work.

Back

With smaller size hook and blue, ch 84 (96, 108).

Row 1 (right side):
Sc in 2nd ch from hook and in each rem ch—83 (95, 107) sc. Ch 3 (counts as first dc on following rows), turn.

Row 2:
Sk first sc, dc in next 4 sc; * ch 1, sk next sc, dc in next 5 sts; rep from * 12 (14, 16) times more, changing to white in last dc. Ch 1, turn.

Row 3:
Sc in first 5 dc; * † working over next ch-1 sp, dc in next skipped sc on 2nd row below †; sc in next 5 dc; rep from * 11 (13, 15) times more, then rep from † to † once; sc in next 4 dc and in 3rd ch of turning ch-3. Ch 3, turn.

Row 4:
Sk first sc, dc in next sc; * ch 1, sk next sc, dc in next 5 sts; rep from * 12 (14, 16) times more; ch 1, sk next sc, dc in next 2 sc, changing to blue in last dc. Ch 1, turn.

continued

Color photograph, page 35

Row 5:
Sc in first 2 dc; * † working over next ch-1 sp, dc in next skipped sc on 2nd row below †; sc in next 5 dc; rep from * 12 (14, 16) times more, then rep from † to † once; sc in next dc and in 3rd ch of turning ch-3. Ch 3, turn.

Rep Rows 2 through 5 until piece measures about 14" from beg, ending by working a Row 5.

Next Row (wrong side):
Sk first sc, dc in next 10 sts; * ch 1, sk next st, dc in next 5 sts; rep from * 9 (11, 13) times more; ch 1, sk next st, dc in next 11 sts. Finish off.

Armhole Shaping:
Hold piece with right side facing you; sk first 6 dc; with white, make lp on hook and join with an sc in next dc.

Row 1 (right side):
Sc in next 4 dc; * working over next ch-1 sp, dc in next skipped sc on 2nd row below, sc in next 5 dc; rep from * 10 (12, 14) times more. Ch 3, turn, leaving rem sts unworked—71 (83, 95) sts.

Row 2:
Sk first sc, dc in next sc; * ch 1, sk next sc, dc in next 5 sts; rep from * 10 (12, 14) times more; ch 1, sk next sc, dc in next 2 sc, changing to blue in last dc. Ch 1, turn.

Row 3:
Sc in first 2 dc; * † working over next ch-1 sp, dc in next skipped sc on 2nd row below †; sc in next 5 dc; rep from * 10 (12, 14) times more, then rep from † to † once; sc in next dc and in 3rd ch of turning ch-3. Ch 3, turn.

Row 4:
Sk first sc, dc in next 4 sts; * ch 1, sk next sc, dc in next 5 sts; rep from * 10 (12, 14) times more, changing to white in last dc. Ch 1, turn.

Row 5:
Sc in first 5 dc; * † working over next ch-1 sp, dc in next skipped sc on 2nd row below †; sc in next 5 dc; rep from * 9 (11, 13) times more, then rep from † to † once; sc in next 4 dc and in 3rd ch of turning ch-3. Ch 3, turn.

Rows 6 through 29 (29, 33):
Rep Rows 2 through 5, 6 (6, 7) times more.

FOR SIZES SMALL AND LARGE ONLY:
Continue with Left Shoulder Shaping.

FOR SIZE MEDIUM ONLY:
Row 30:
Rep Row 2.

Row 31:
Rep Row 3.

Continue with Left Shoulder Shaping.

Left Shoulder Shaping:
FOR SIZES SMALL AND LARGE ONLY:
Row 1 (wrong side):
Sk first sc, dc in next sc; * ch 1, sk next dc, dc in next 5 sts; rep from * 2 (4) times more, changing to blue in last dc. Ch 1, turn, leaving rem sts unworked.

Row 2 (right side):
Sc in first 5 dc; * † working over next ch-1 sp, dc in next skipped sc on 2nd row below †; sc in next 5 dc; rep from * 1 (3) times more, then rep from † to † once; sc in next dc and in 3rd ch of turning ch-3—20 (32) sts. Finish off.

Continue with Right Shoulder Shaping below.

FOR SIZE MEDIUM ONLY:
Row 1 (wrong side):
Sk first sc, dc in next 4 sts; * ch 1, sk next sc, dc in next 5 sts; rep from * twice more; ch 1, sk next sc, dc in next 2 sc, changing to white in last dc. Ch 1, turn, leaving rem sts unworked.

Row 2 (right side):
Sc in first 2 dc; * † working over next ch-1 sp, dc in next skipped sc on 2nd row below †; sc in next 5 dc; rep from * twice more, then rep from † to † once; sc in next 4 dc and in 3rd ch of turning ch-3—26 sts. Finish off.

Continue with Right Shoulder Shaping.

Right Shoulder Shaping:
FOR SIZES SMALL AND LARGE ONLY:
Hold Back with wrong side facing you; sk next 31 sts from left shoulder shaping, join white in next dc.

Row 1 (wrong side):
Ch 3 (counts as a dc), dc in next 4 sts; * ch 1, sk next sc, dc in next 5 sts; rep from * 1 (3) times more; ch 1, sk next sc, dc in next 2 dc, changing to blue in last dc. Ch 1, turn.

Row 2 (right side):
Sc in first 2 sc; * † working over next ch-1 sp, dc in next skipped sc on 2nd row below †; sc in next 5 dc; rep from * 1 (3) times more, then rep from † to † once; dc in next 4 dc and in 3rd ch of turning ch-3—20 (32) sts. Finish off.

FOR SIZE MEDIUM ONLY:
Hold Back with wrong side facing you; sk next 31 sts from left shoulder shaping, join blue in next dc.

Row 1 (wrong side):
Ch 3 (counts as a dc), dc in next sc; * ch 1, sk next sc, dc in next 5 sts; rep from * 3 times more, changing to white in last dc. Ch 1, turn.

Row 2 (right side):
Sc in first 5 dc; * † working over next ch-1 sp, dc in next skipped sc on 2nd row below †; sc in next 5 dc; rep from * twice more, then rep from † to † once; sc in next dc and in 3rd ch of turning ch-3—26 sts. Finish off.

Front

Work same as Back through Row 5 of armhole shaping.

Rows 6 through 9 (9, 13):
Rep Rows 2 through 5, once (once, twice) more.

Row 10 (10, 14):
Rep Row 2.

Left Neck and Shoulder Shaping:

Row 1 (right side):
Work in pattern as established across first 35 (41, 47) sts. Ch 3, turn, leaving rem sts unworked.

Row 2:
Sk first sc, dec over next 2 sts [to work dec: (YO, draw up lp in next st, YO and draw through 2 lps on hook) twice; YO and draw through all 3 lps on hook—dec made]; work in patt across—34 (40, 46) sts. Ch 1, turn.

Row 3:
Work in patt to last 2 dc and turning ch-3; sc dec over next 2 dc (to work sc dec: draw up lp in each of next 2 dc, YO and draw through all 3 lps on hook—sc dec made); sc in 3rd ch of turning ch-3—33 (39, 45) sts. Ch 3, turn.

Rows 4 through 15:
Rep Rows 2 and 3 six times more. At end of Row 15—21 (27, 33) sts.

Row 16:
Rep Row 2. At end of row—20 (26, 32) sts.

Work even in color sequence and pattern as established until armhole has same number of rows as Back, ending by working a right side row. Finish off.

Right Neck and Shoulder Shaping:

Hold Front with right side facing you; sk next unused dc from left neck, working in color sequence and pattern as established, make lp on hook and join with an sc in next dc.

Row 1 (right side):
Work in pattern as established across—35 (41, 47) sts. Ch 3, turn.

Row 2:
Work in patt to last 3 sts; dec over next 2 sts; dc in next sc—34 (40, 46) sts. Ch 1, turn.

Row 3:
Sc in first dc, sc dec over next 2 dc; work in patt across—33 (39, 45) sts. Ch 3, turn.

Rows 4 through 15:
Rep Rows 2 and 3 six times more. At end of Row 15—21 (27, 33) sts.

Row 16:
Rep Row 2. At end of row—20 (26, 32) sts.

Work even in color sequence and pattern as established until armhole has same number of rows as Back, ending by working a right side row. Finish off.

Sleeve (make 2)

With smaller size hook and blue, ch 60 (60, 66).

Row 1 (right side):
Sc in 2nd ch from hook and in each rem ch—59 (59, 65) sc. Ch 3 (counts as first dc on following rows), turn.

Row 2:
Dc in first 5 sc; * ch 1, sk next sc, dc in next 5 sc; rep from * 7 (7, 8) times more; ch 1, sk next sc, dc in next 4 sc, 2 dc in next sc, changing to white in last dc—61 (61, 67) sts. Ch 1, turn.

For Size Small Only:

Row 3:
Sc in first 6 dc; * working over next ch-1 sp, dc in next skipped sc on 2nd row below; sc in next 5 dc; rep from * 8 times more; sc in 3rd ch of turning ch-3. Ch 3, turn.

Row 4:
Dc in first 3 sc; * ch 1, sk next sc, dc in next 5 sts; rep from * 8 times more; ch 1, sk next sc, dc in next 2 sc, 2 dc in next sc, changing to blue in last dc—63 sts. Ch 1, turn.

Row 5:
Sc in first 4 dc; * † working over next ch-1 sp, dc in next skipped sc on 2nd row below †; sc in next 5 dc; rep from * 8 times more, then rep from † to † once; sc in next 3 dc and in 3rd ch of turning ch-3. Ch 3, turn.

Row 6:
Dc in first sc; * ch 1, sk next sc, dc in next 5 sts; rep from * 9 times more; ch 1, sk next sc, 2 dc in next sc, changing to white in last dc—65 sts. Ch 1, turn.

Rows 7 through 22:
Continue to work in color sequence and pattern as established, inc one st each side every other row 8 times. At end of Row 22—81 sts.

Rows 23 through 25:
Work even in pattern.

Row 26:
Dc in each sc and in each ch-1 sp.

Finish off and weave in all ends.

For Sizes Medium and Large Only:

Row 3:
2 sc in first dc; sc in next 5 dc; * working over next ch-1 sp, dc in next skipped sc on 2nd row below; sc in next 5 dc; rep from * 8 (9) times more; 2 sc in 3rd ch of turning ch-3—63 (69) sts. Ch 3, turn.

continued

53

Row 4:
Dc in first 4 sc; * ch 1, sk next sc, dc in next 5 sts; rep from * 8 (9) times more; ch 1, sk next sc, dc in next 3 sc, 2 dc in next sc, changing to blue in last dc—65 (71) sts. Ch 1, turn.

Row 5:
2 sc in first dc; sc in next 4 dc; * † working over next ch-1 sp, dc in next skipped sc on 2nd row below †; dc in next 5 dc; rep from * 8 (9) times more, then rep from † to † once; dc in next 4 dc, 2 sc in 3rd ch of turning ch-3—67 (73) sts. Ch 3, turn.

Row 6:
Dc in first 3 sc; * ch 1, sk next sc, dc in next 5 sts; rep from * 9 (10) times more; ch 1, sk next sc, dc in next 2 sc, 2 dc in next sc, changing to blue in last dc—69 (75) sts. Ch 1, turn.

Row 7:
Sc in first 4 dc; * † working over next ch-1 sp, dc in next skipped sc on 2nd row below †; dc in next 5 dc; rep from * 9 (10) times more, then rep from † to † once; dc in next 3 dc and in 3rd ch of turning ch-3. Ch 3, turn.

Rows 8 through 22:
Continue to work in color sequence and pattern as established, inc one st each side every other row 8 times. At end of Row 22—85 (91) sts.

Rows 23 through 25:
Work even in pattern.

Row 26:
Dc in each sc and in each ch-1 sp.

Finish off and weave in all ends.

Sew shoulder seams.

Neck Band
Hold sweater with right side facing you and right shoulder at top; with smaller size hook, join blue in right shoulder seam.

Rnd 1 (right side):
Ch 3, working along back right neck edge, dc in edge sc of next row, 3 dc in sp formed by edge dc of next row; working across back neck edge, dc in next 31 sts; working along back left neck edge, 3 dc in sp formed by edge dc of next row; dc in edge sc of next row and in left shoulder seam; working along left front neck edge in sps formed by edge dc, 3 dc in each dc row; keeping last lp of each dc on

hook, dc in last dc of left shoulder, in center skipped dc, and in first dc of right shoulder; YO and draw through all 4 lps on hook; working along right neck edge in sps formed by edge dc, 3 dc in each dc row; join in 3rd ch of beg ch-3.

Change to larger size hook.

Rnd 2:
Sl st in each dc; join in joining sl st.

Finish off and weave in ends.

Finishing
Step 1:
Referring to diagram, sew Sleeves in armhole openings between A and B, having center of Sleeves at shoulder seams and easing as necessary to fit.

Step 2:
Beginning at B and carefully matching color pattern, sew sleeve seams. Sew side seams matching color pattern.

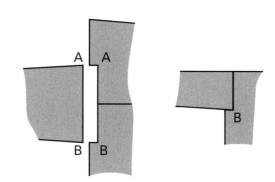

Shells and Mesh Sweater

designed by Sandy Scoville

Sizes:

	Small	Medium	Large
Chest Measurement:	30"-32"	34"-36"	38"-40"
Finished Chest Measurement:	40"	44"	48"

Note: Instructions are written for size small; changes for larger sizes are in parentheses.

Materials:

Lion Brand Wool-Ease (3 oz skein), 7 (8, 9) skeins Fisherman #99; one skein Black #153—or other worsted weight yarn worked to gauge
Size I (5.5mm) crochet hook, or size required for gauge
Size 16 tapestry needle

Gauge:

Note: See "A Word about Gauge" on page 5.
7 hdc = 2"
4 hdc rows = 1½"

Pattern Stitch

Front Post Double Crochet (FPdc):
YO, insert hook from front to back to front around post (see Stitch Guide on page 5) of next hdc on 2nd row below, draw lp through, (YO, draw through 2 lps on hook) twice—FPdc maded.

Note: On working row, sk hdc behind FPdc.

Instructions

Back

With off white, ch 72 (78, 84).

Row 1 (right side):
Hdc in 3rd ch from hook (beg 2 skipped chs count as an hdc) and in each rem ch—71 (77, 83) hdc. Ch 2 (counts as first hdc on following rows), turn.

Row 2:
Sk first hdc, hdc in next hdc; * ch 1, sk next hdc, hdc in next hdc; rep from * to beg 2 skipped chs; hdc in 2nd ch of beg 2 skipped chs—34 (37, 40) ch-1 sps. Ch 3 (counts as first hdc and ch-1 sp on following rows), turn.

Row 3:
Sk first 2 hdc; * hdc in next ch-1 sp, ch 1; rep from * to last hdc and turning ch-2; sk last hdc, hdc in 2nd ch of turning ch-2—35 (38, 41) ch-1 sps. Ch 2, turn.

Row 4:
Sk first hdc, hdc in next ch-1 sp; * ch 1, hdc in next ch-1 sp; rep from * to last hdc and turning ch-3; ch 1, sk last hdc, hdc in next 2 chs of turning ch-3—34 (37, 40) ch-1 sps. Ch 2, turn.

Row 5:
Sk first hdc, hdc in each rem hdc, in each ch-1 sp, and in 2nd ch of turning ch-2—71 (77, 83) hdc. Ch 2, turn.

continued

All measurements are approximate.

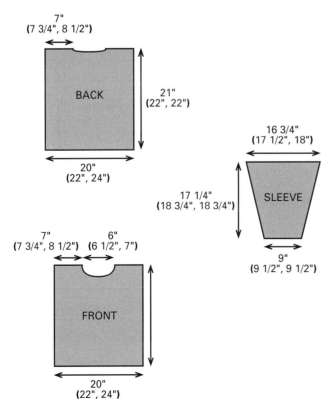

Color photograph, page 33

55

Row 6:
Sk first hdc, hdc in each rem hdc and in 2nd ch of turning ch-2. Ch 2, turn.

Rows 7 and 8:
Rep Row 6. At end of Row 8, do not ch 2; draw up 6" long loop and remove hook; drop off white. Turn.

Trim Row:
With black, make lp on hook and join in FL of first hdc at beg of Row 8; working in FLs only, loosely sl st in next 4 hdc, FPdc (see Pattern Stitch on page 55) around post of next hdc on 2nd row below; * sl st in next 5 hdc, FPdc around post of next hdc on 2nd row below; rep from * 9 (10, 11) times more; sl st in next 4 hdc and in one lp of 2nd ch of turning ch-2. Finish off black. Turn and insert hook in long off white loop; pull yarn to tighten. Ch 2, turn.

Note: On following row you will work again into FLs as well as BLs of sts used on trim row.

Row 9:
Working behind trim row through both lps of hdc and skipped hdc on Row 8 (including lps already worked for trim row), sk first hdc, hdc in each rem hdc and in 2nd ch of turning ch-2—71 (77, 83) hdc. Ch 2, turn.

Rows 10:
Sk first hdc, hdc in each rem hdc and in 2nd ch of turning ch-2. Ch 2, turn.

Rows 11 and 12:
Rep Row 10.

Row 13:
Sk first hdc, hdc in next hdc; * ch 1, sk next hdc, hdc in next hdc; rep from * to turning ch-2; hdc in 2nd ch of turning ch-2. Ch 3, turn.

Rows 14 and 15:
Rep Rows 3 and 4.

Row 16:
Sk first hdc, hdc in next hdc, 2 hdc in each of next 34 (37, 40) ch-1 sps; sk next hdc, hdc in 2nd ch of turning ch-2—71 (77, 83) hdc. Ch 1, turn.

Row 17:
Sc in first hdc; * sk next 2 hdc, 5 dc in next hdc—shell made; sk next 2 hdc, sc in next hdc; rep from * 10 (11, 12) times more; sk next 2 hdc, 3 dc in next hdc—11 (12, 13) shells. Ch 1, turn, leaving turning ch-2 unworked.

Row 18:
Sc in first dc, shell in next sc; * sc in 3rd dc of next shell, shell in next sc; rep from * 9 (10, 11) times more; sc in 3rd dc of next shell, 3 dc in next sc. Ch 1, turn.

Row 19:
Sc in first dc; * shell in next sc; sc in 3rd dc of next shell; rep from * 10 (11, 12) times more; 3 dc in next sc. Ch 1, turn.

Row 20:
Rep Row 19.

Row 21:
Sc in first dc, ch 2, hdc in next sc; * ch 2, sc in 3rd dc of next shell, ch 2, hdc in next sc; rep from * 10 (11, 12) times more. Ch 2, turn.

Row 22:
Hdc in first hdc; * 2 hdc in next ch-2 sp; hdc in next sc, 2 hdc in next ch-2 sp; hdc in next hdc; rep from * 10 (11, 12) times more; 2 hdc in next ch-2 sp; hdc in next sc—71 (77, 83) sts. Ch 2, turn.

Row 23:
Sk first hdc; * hdc in next hdc, ch 1, sk next hdc; rep from * to last hdc and turning ch-2; hdc in last hdc and in 2nd ch of turning ch-2. Ch 3, turn.

Rows 24 through 29:
Rep Rows 3 through 8. At end of Row 29, do not ch 2, do not turn. Draw up 6" long loop and remove hook; drop off white.

Trim Row:
With black, make lp on hook and join in FL of 2nd ch of turning ch-2 at beg of Row 29; working in FLs only, loosely sl st in next 4 hdc, FPdc around next hdc on 2nd row below; * sl st in next 5 hdc, FPdc around next hdc on 2nd row below; rep from * 9 (10, 11) times more; sl st in next 5 hdc. Finish off black. Insert hook in long off white loop; pull yarn to tighten. Ch 2, turn.

Note: On following row you will work again into FLs as well as BLs of sts used on trim row.

Row 30:
Working in front of trim row through both lps of hdc and skipped hdc on Row 29 (including lps already worked for trim row), sk first hdc, hdc in each rem hdc and in 2nd ch of turning ch-2. Ch 2, turn.

Rows 31 through 40:
Rep Rows 10 through 19.

Rows 41 through 43:
Rep Rows 21 through 23.

Rows 44 through 46:
Rep Rows 3 through 5.

Row 47:
Sk first hdc, hdc in each rem hdc and in 2nd ch of turning ch-2. Ch 2, turn.

Rows 48 through 53 (55, 55):
Rep Row 47.

Row 54 (56, 56):
Sk first hdc, hdc in next hdc; * ch 1, sk next hdc, hdc in next hdc; rep from * to turning ch-2; hdc in 2nd ch of turning ch-2. Ch 3, turn.

Row 55 (57, 57):
Sk first 2 hdc; * hdc in next ch-1 sp, ch 1; rep from * to last hdc and turning ch-2; sk last hdc, hdc in 2nd ch of turning ch-2. Ch 2, turn.

Left Back Shoulder and Neckline Shaping:
Row 1 (wrong side):
Sk first hdc; * hdc in next ch-1 sp, ch 1; rep from * 11 (12, 13) times more; dec over next ch-1 sp and next hdc (to work dec: YO, draw up lp in next ch-1 sp, YO, draw up lp in next hdc; YO and draw through all 5 lps on hook—dec made)—12 (13, 14) ch-1 sps. Ch 2, turn, leaving rem sts unworked.

Row 2 (right side):
Sk first st and next ch-1 sp, hdc in each hdc, in each ch-1 sp, and in 2nd ch of turning ch-2—25 (27, 29) hdc. Finish off.

Right Back Shoulder and Neckline Shaping:
Hold Back with wrong side facing you and Row 55 (57, 57) at top; sk next 9 (10, 11) ch-1 sps from left shoulder, join off white in next hdc.

Row 1 (wrong side):
Ch 3 (counts as an hdc and a ch-1 sp), sk next hdc; * hdc in next ch-1 sp, ch 1; rep from * 10 (11, 12) times more; hdc in next 2 chs of turning ch-3—12 (13, 14) ch-1 sps. Ch 2, turn.

Row 2 (right side):
Sk first hdc; * hdc in next hdc and in next ch-1 sp; rep from * 10 (11, 12) times more; hdc in next hdc, sk next ch of beg ch-3, hdc in next ch—25 (27, 29) hdc. Finish off.

Front
With off white, ch 72 (78, 84).

Rows 1 through 53 (55, 55):
Rep Rows 1 through 53 (55, 55) of Back.

For Size Small:
On Row 52, mark 27th, 33rd, 39th, and 45th st for neck trim.

For Size Medium:
On Row 54, mark 30th, 36th, 42nd, and 48th st for neck trim.

For Size Large:
On Row 54, mark 33rd, 39th, 45th, and 51st st for neck trim.

Right Front Shoulder and Neckline Shaping:
Row 1 (wrong side):
Sk first hdc, hdc in next hdc; * ch 1, sk next hdc, hdc in next hdc; rep from * 10 (11, 12) times more; ch 1, sk next hdc, dec over next 2 hdc [to work dec: (YO, draw up lp in next hdc) twice; YO and draw through all 5 lps on hook—dec made]—12 (13, 14) ch-1 sps. Ch 2, turn, leaving rem sts unworked.

Row 2 (right side):
Sk first st; * hdc in next ch-1 sp, ch 1; rep from * 11 (12, 13) times more; hdc in 2nd ch of turning ch-2. Ch 2, turn.

Row 3:
Sk first hdc; * hdc in next ch-1 sp, ch 1; rep from * 11 (12, 13) times more; hdc in 2nd ch of turning ch-2—12 (13, 14) ch-1 sps. Ch 2, turn.

Row 4:
Sk first hdc and next ch-1 sp; * hdc in each rem hdc, in each ch-1 sp, and in 2nd ch of turning ch-2—25 (27, 29) hdc. Finish off.

Left Front Shoulder and Neckline Shaping:
Hold Front with wrong side facing you and Row 53 (55, 55) at top; sk next 17 (19, 21) hdc from right shoulder, join off white in next hdc.

Row 1 (wrong side):
Ch 3 (counts as an hdc and a ch-1 sp), sk next hdc, dec over next 2 hdc; * ch 1, sk next hdc, hdc in next hdc; rep from * 10 (11, 12) times more; hdc in 2nd ch of turning ch-2—12 (13, 14) ch-1 sps. Ch 3 (counts as first hdc and ch-1 sp on following rows), turn.

Row 2 (right side):
Sk first 2 hdc; * hdc in next ch-1 sp, ch 1; rep from * 10 (11, 12) times more; hdc in next 2 chs of beg ch-3. Ch 3, turn.

Row 3:
Sk first 2 hdc; * hdc in next ch-1 sp, ch 1; rep from * 10 (11, 12) times more; hdc in next 2 chs of turning ch-3—12 (13, 14) ch-1 sps. Ch 2, turn.

Row 4:
Sk first hdc; * hdc in each rem hdc, and in each ch-1 sp to turning ch-3; sk next ch of turning ch-3, hdc in next ch—25 (27, 29) hdc. Finish off.

Sleeve (make 2)
With off white, ch 32 (34, 34).

Row 1 (right side):
Hdc in 3rd ch from hook (beg 2 skipped chs count as an hdc) and in each rem ch—31 (33, 33) hdc. Ch 2 (counts as first hdc on following rows), turn.

Row 2:
Sk first hdc, hdc in each rem hdc and in 2nd ch of beg 2 skipped chs. Ch 2, turn.

Row 3:
Sk first hdc, hdc in each rem hdc and in 2nd ch of turning ch-2. Ch 2, turn.

Row 4:
Hdc in first hdc and in each rem hdc to turning ch-2; 2 hdc in 2nd ch of turning ch-2—33 (35, 35) hdc. Ch 2, turn.

continued

Rows 5 through 8:
Rep Rows 3 and 4 twice more. At end of Row 8—37 (39, 39) hdc. Ch 3 (counts as first hdc and ch-1 sp on following rows), turn.

Row 9:
Sk first 2 hdc; * hdc in next hdc, ch 1, sk next hdc; rep from * to turning ch-2; hdc in 2nd ch of turning ch-2—18 (19, 19) ch-1 sps. Ch 2, turn.

Row 10:
Hdc in first hdc and in next ch-1 sp, ch 1; * hdc in next ch-1 sp, ch 1; rep from * to turning ch-3; hdc in next ch of turning ch-3, 2 hdc in next ch of turning ch—17 (18, 18) ch-1 sps. Ch 2, turn.

Row 11:
Sk first hdc, hdc in next hdc; * ch 1, hdc in next ch-1 sp; rep from * to last 2 hdc and turning ch-2; ch 1, sk next hdc, hdc next hdc and in 2nd ch of turning ch-2—18 (19, 19) ch-1 sps. Ch 2, turn.

Row 12:
Hdc in first hdc, in each rem hdc and in each ch-1 sp to turning ch-2; 2 hdc in 2nd ch of turning ch-2—41 (43, 43) hdc. Ch 2, turn.

Row 13:
Sk first hdc, hdc in each rem hdc and in 2nd ch of turning ch-2. Ch 2, turn.

Row 14:
Hdc in first hdc and in each rem hdc to turning ch-2; 2 hdc in 2nd ch of turning ch-2—43 (45, 45) hdc. Ch 2, turn.

Row 15:
Sk first hdc, hdc in each hdc and in 2nd ch of turning ch-2. Do not turn. Draw up 6" long loop and remove hook; drop off white.

Trim Row:
With black, make lp on hook and join in FL of 2nd ch of turning ch-2 at beg of Row 15; working in FLs only, loosely sl st in next 2 (3, 3) hdc; FPdc around next hdc on 2nd row below; * sl st in next 5 hdc, FPdc around next hdc fon 2nd row below; rep from * 5 (5, 5) times more; sl st in next 3 (4, 4) hdc. Finish off black. Insert hook in long off white loop; pull yarn to tighten. Ch 2, turn.

Note: On following row you will work again into FLs as well as BLs of sts used on trim row.

Row 16:
Working behind trim row through both lps of hdc and skipped hdc on Row 15 (including lps already worked for trim row), hdc in first hdc and in each rem hdc to turning ch-2, 2 hdc in 2nd ch of turning ch-2—45 (47, 47) hdc. Ch 2, turn.

Rows 17 and 18:
Rep Rows 13 and 14. At end of Row 18—47 (49, 49) hdc. Ch 3, turn.

Row 19:
Sk first 2 hdc; * hdc in next hdc, ch 1, sk next hdc; rep from * to turning ch-2; hdc in 2nd ch of turning ch-2—23 (24, 24) ch-1 sps. Ch 2, turn.

Row 20:
Hdc in first hdc; * hdc in next ch-1 sp, ch 1; rep from * to turning ch-3; hdc in next ch of turning ch, 2 hdc in next ch—22 (23, 23) ch-1 sps. Ch 2, turn.

Row 21:
Sk first hdc, hdc in next hdc, ch 1; * hdc in next ch-1 sp, ch 1; rep from * to last 2 hdc and turning ch-2; sk next hdc, hdc in next hdc and in 2nd ch of turning ch-2—23 (24, 24) ch-1 sps. Ch 2, turn.

Row 22:
Hdc in first hdc, 2 hdc in each of next 23 (24, 24) ch-1 sps; hdc in next hdc, 2 hdc in 2nd ch of turning ch-2—51 (53, 53) hdc. Ch 1, turn.

For Size Small Only:
Row 23:
Sc in first 2 hdc, sk next 2 hdc, 5 dc in next hdc—shell made; sk next 2 hdc; * sc in next hdc, sk next 2 hdc, 5 dc in next hdc—shell made; sk next 2 hdc; rep from * 6 times more; sc in next hdc and in 2nd ch of turning ch-2—8 shells. Ch 1, turn.

Row 24:
Sc in first sc, 3 dc in next sc; * sc in 3rd dc of next shell, shell in next sc; rep from * 6 times more; sc in 3rd dc of next shell, 3 dc in next sc; sc in next sc—7 shells. Ch 1, turn.

Row 25:
Sc in first 2 sts; * shell in next sc; sc in 3rd dc of next shell; rep from * 6 times more; shell in next sc; sk next 2 dc, sc next 2 sts—8 shells. Ch 1, turn.

Row 26:
Rep Row 24.

Row 27:
Sc in first 2 sts, ch 2, hdc in next sc, ch 2; * sc in 3rd dc of next shell, ch 2, hdc in next sc, ch 2; rep from * 6 times more; sk next 2 dc, sc in next 2 sts—16 ch-2 sps. Ch 2, turn.

Row 28:
Hdc in first 2 sc; 2 hdc in next ch-2 sp; * hdc in next st, 2 hdc in next ch-2 sp; rep from * 14 times more; hdc in next sc, 2 hdc in next sc—53 hdc. Ch 2, turn.

Continue with For All Sizes on page 59.

For Size Medium Only:
Row 23:
Sc in first 3 hdc, sk next 2 hdc, 5 dc in next hdc—shell made; sk next 2 hdc; * sc in next hdc, sk next 2 hdc, 5 dc in next hdc—shell made; sk next 2 hdc; rep from * 6 times more; sc in next 2 hdc and in 2nd ch of turning ch-2—8 shells. Ch 1, turn.

Row 24:
Sc in first 2 sc, 3 dc in next sc; * sc in 3rd dc of next shell, shell in next sc; rep from * 6 times more; sc in 3rd dc of next shell, 3 dc in next sc; sc in next 2 sc—7 shells. Ch 1, turn.

Row 25:
Sc in first 2 sc and in next dc; shell in next sc; * sc in 3rd dc of next shell, shell in next sc; rep from * 6 times more; sk next 2 dc, sc in next dc and in next 2 sc—8 shells. Ch 1, turn.

Row 26:
Sc in first 2 sc, 3 dc in next sc; * sc in 3rd dc of next shell, shell in next sc; rep from * 6 times more; sc in 3rd dc of next shell, 3 dc in next sc; sc in next 2 sc. Ch 3 (counts as an hdc and a ch-1 sp on following row), turn.

Row 27:
Sk first 2 sc, sc in next dc, ch 2, sk next 2 dc; * hdc in next sc, ch 2, sc in 3rd dc of next shell, ch 2; rep from * 6 times more; hdc in next sc, ch 2, sk next 2 dc, sc in next dc, ch 1, sk next sc, hdc in next sc. Ch 2, turn.

Row 28:
Hdc in first hdc, in next ch-1 sp, and in next sc; * 2 hdc in next ch-2 sp; hdc in next st; rep from * 15 times more; hdc in next ch of turning ch-3, 2 hdc in next ch of turning ch—55 hdc. Ch 2, turn.

Continue with For All Sizes.

For Size Large Only:
Row 23:
Sc in first 3 hdc, sk next 2 hdc, 5 dc in next hdc—shell made; sk next 2 hdc; * sc in next hdc, sk next 2 hdc, 5 dc in next hdc—shell made; sk next 2 hdc; rep from * 6 times more; sc in next 2 hdc and in 2nd ch of turning ch-2—8 shells. Ch 1, turn.

Row 24:
Sc in first sc, sk next sc, shell in next sc; * sc in 3rd dc of next shell, shell in next sc; rep from * 7 times more; sk next sc, sc in next sc—9 shells. Ch 3 (counts as first dc on following rows), turn.

Row 25:
2 dc in first sc; * sc in 3rd dc of next shell, shell in next sc; rep from * 7 times more; sc in 3rd dc of next shell, 3 dc in next sc—8 shells. Ch 1, turn.

Row 26:
Sc in first dc, shell in next sc; * sc in 3rd dc of next shell, shell in next sc; rep from * 7 times more; sc in 3rd ch of turning ch-3—9 shells. Ch 4 (counts as first hdc and ch-2 sp on following rows), turn.

Row 27:
* Sc in 3rd dc of next shell, ch 2, hdc in next sc, ch 2; rep from * 7 times more; sc in 3rd dc of next shell, ch 2, hdc in next sc—18 ch-2 sps. Ch 2, turn.

Row 28:
Hdc in first hdc, 2 hdc in next ch-2 sp; * hdc in next st, 2 hdc in next ch-2 sp; rep from * 16 times more; sk next 2 chs of turning ch-4, 2 hdc in next ch—57 hdc. Ch 2, turn.

Continue with For All Sizes.

For All Sizes:
Row 29:
Sk first hdc; * hdc in next hdc, ch 1, sk next hdc; rep from * 24 (25, 26) times more; hdc in next hdc and in 2nd ch of turning ch-2—25 (26, 27) ch-1 sps. Ch 3, turn.

Row 30:
* Hdc in next ch-1 sp, ch 1; rep from * 24 (25, 26) times more; hdc in 2nd ch of turning ch-2—26 (27, 28) ch-1 sps. Ch 2, turn.

Row 31:
* Hdc in next ch-1 sp, ch 1; rep from * 24 (25, 26) times more; sk next hdc, hdc in next 2 chs of turning ch-3—25 (26, 27) ch-1 sps. Ch 2, turn.

Row 32:
Hdc in first hdc, in each rem hdc, and in each ch-1 sp to turning ch-2; 2 hdc in 2nd ch of turning ch-2—55 (57, 59) hdc. Ch 2, turn.

Row 33:
Sk first hdc, hdc in each rem hdc and in 2nd ch of turning ch-2. Ch 2, turn.

Rows 34 and 35:
Rep Row 33. At end of Row 35, do not ch 2; do not turn. Draw up 6" long loop and remove hook; drop off white.

Trim Row:
With black, make lp on hook and join in FL of 2nd ch of beg ch-2 at beg of Row 35; working in FLs only, loosely sl st in next 2 (3, 4) hdc, FPdc around next hdc on 2nd row below; * sl st in next 5 hdc, FPdc around next hdc on 2nd row below; rep from * 7 (7, 7) times more; sl st in next 3 (4, 5) hdc. Finish off black. Insert hook in long off white loop; pull yarn to tighten. Ch 2, turn.

Note: On following row you will work again into FLs as well as BLs of sts used on trim row.

Row 36:
Working in back of trim row through both lps of hdc and skipped hdc on Row 35 (including lps already worked for trim row), hdc in first hdc and in each rem hdc to turning ch-2; 2 hdc in 2nd ch of turning ch-2—57 (59, 61) hdc. Ch 2, turn.

Row 37:
Sk first hdc, hdc in each rem hdc and in 2nd ch of turning ch-2. Ch 2, turn.

continued

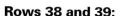

Rows 38 and 39:
Rep Row 37.

Row 40:
Hdc first hdc; * ch 1, sk next hdc, hdc in next hdc; rep from * 27 (28, 29) times more; ch 1, sk next hdc, 2 hdc in 2nd ch of turning ch-2—28 (29, 30) ch-1 sps. Ch 3, turn.

Row 41:
* Hdc in next ch-1 sp, ch 1; rep from * 27 (28, 29) times more; hdc in 2nd ch of turning ch-2—29 (30, 31) ch-1 sps. Ch 2, turn.

Row 42:
* Hdc in next ch-1 sp, ch 1; rep from * 27 (28, 29) times more; hdc in next 2 chs of turning ch-3—28 (29, 30) ch-1 sps. Ch 2, turn.

Row 43:
Sk first hdc, hdc in each rem hdc, in each ch-1 sp, and in 2nd ch of turning ch-2—59 (61, 63) hdc. Ch 2, turn.

Row 44:
Sk first hdc, hdc in each rem hdc and in 2nd ch of turning ch-2. Ch 2, turn.

Rows 45 and 46:
Rep Row 44.

For Size Small Only:
Finish off and weave in all ends.

For Sizes Medium and Large Only:
Rows 47 through 50:
Rep Row 44.

Finish off and weave in all ends.

Sew shoulder seams, carefully matching stitches.

Neckline Trim

For Size Small Only:
Hold sweater with right side of front facing you and left shoulder seam at top; with black, make lp on hook and join with an sc in left shoulder seam; working along left front neck edge in sps formed by edge hdc and turning chs, sc in next 4 rows; FPdc around first marked st on Row 52 of front; working across front in unused hdc, * sc in next 5 hdc, FPdc around next marked st on Row 52; on working row, sk next sc; rep from * once more; on working row, sc in next 5 hdc, FPdc around next marked st on Row 52; working along right front neck edge in sps formed by edge hdc and turning chs, sc in next 4 rows and in right shoulder seam; working along right back neck edge in sps formed by edge hdc and turning ch, sc in next 2 rows; working across back, (sc in next ch-1 sp and in next hdc) 8 times; sc in next ch-1 sp; working along left back neck edge in sps formed by edge hdc and turning ch, sc in next 2 rows; join in first sc—50 sts.

Finish off and weave in ends.

For Size Medium Only:
Hold sweater with right side of front facing you and left shoulder seam at top; with black, make lp on hook and join with an sc in left shoulder seam; working along left front neck edge in sps formed by edge hdc and turning chs, sc in next 4 rows, FPdc around first marked st on Row 54 of front; working across front in unused hdc, * sc in next 5 hdc, FPdc around next marked st on Row 54; rep from * twice more; working along right front neck edge in sps formed by edge hdc and turning chs, sc in next 4 rows and in right shoulder seam; working along right back neck edge in sps formed by edge hdc and turning ch, sc in next 2 rows; working across back, (sc in next ch-1 sp and in next hdc) 9 times; sc in next ch-1 sp; working along left back neck edge in sps formed by edge hdc and turning ch, sc in next 2 rows; join in first sc—52 sts.

Finish off and weave in ends.

For Size Large Only:
Hold sweater with right side of front facing you and left shoulder seam at top; with black, make lp on hook and join with an sc in left shoulder seam; working along left front neck edge in sps formed by edge hdc and turning chs, sc in next 4 rows; working across front neck edge in unused hdc, sc in next hdc, FPdc around first marked st on Row 54 of front; * sc in next 5 hdc, FPdc around next marked st on Row 54; rep from * twice more; on working row, sc in next hdc; working along right front neck edge in sps formed by edge hdc and turning chs, sc in next 4 rows and in right shoulder seam; working along right back neck edge in sps formed by edge hdc and turning ch, sc in next 2 rows; working across back, (sc in next ch-1 sp and in next hdc) 10 times; sc in next ch-1 sp; working along left back neck edge in sps formed by edge hdc and turning ch, sc in next 2 rows; join in first sc—56 sts.

Finish off and weave in ends.

Finishing
Step 1:
Measusre 8 1/2" (9", 9") on each side of shoulder seam and place markers on armhole edge. Sew Sleeves between markers, easing to fit.

Step 2:
Sew sleeve and side seams, matching pattern.